'A talented, imaginative and unique writer' *The Times*

'Linguistic virtuosity that, at its best, is heady and acrobatic' *New York Times*

'Richly lyrical and inventive ... Mr Nolan is undoubtedly an author of rare gifts' *Independent*

'Brilliantly precise and concrete observation'
Daily Telegraph

'A vigorous and impressive literary performance' *TLS*

'He has a keen sense of the generations of mute, helpless cripples who have been "dashed, branded and treated as dross" for want of a voice to tell us what it feels like. Now that voice ... has come, and we know'
John Carey

'Battling against the cruellest handicaps, he has produced a book of sheer wonder' *Daily Express*

Christopher Nolan was born and still lives in Ireland. He was educated in Dublin at the Central Remedial Clinic School, Mount Temple Comprehensive and Trinity College. He published his first book, *Dam-Burst of Dreams*, a collection of poetry and other writings, ('a jubilant, lawless debut' – John Carey) in 1981. In 1987 *Under the Eye of the Clock* won the Whitbread Book of the Year Award.

By the same author

Dam-Burst of Dreams
The Banyan Tree

Under the Eye of the Clock

THE LIFE STORY OF
CHRISTOPHER NOLAN

PREFACE BY
JOHN CAREY

PHŒNIX

A Phoenix Paperback
First published in Great Britain by Weidenfeld & Nicolson in 1987
This paperback edition published in 1999 by Phoenix,
an imprint of Orion Books Ltd,
Orion House, 5 Upper St Martin's Lane,
London WC2H 9EA

A CIP catalogue record for this book
is available from the British Library.

ISBN: 0 75380 709 2

Printed and bound in Great Britain by
The Guernsey Press Co. Ltd,
Guernsey, C.I.

A CHILD'S REMEMBERING.

Chimes, ago in 'Gortnamona',
Nimbly gong bold ding dong,
Pummelled in my brain, bespoked,
They burrow now and still.

Playing then and playing now
Mobile-notioned ladders,
I climb up and slither back
My very chastened chiming.

Baby then but fifteen months,
I chance home often there,
Never physically to return,
My new home, a farm elsewhere.

But back I go and dwell awhile
Cosy kitchen in Rathgowan,
The wallpaper basket-woven,
The presses painted green.

Bubbling memory vests the layout,
Childlike as in a dream,
My momentary mental visit
Blinks awake on a false ding dong.

CONTENTS

CONTENTS

PREFACE

A new book by Christy Nolan does not need a preface by me or anyone, but he has asked me to write one and I am glad to. His first book, *Dam-Burst of Dreams*, was a jubilant, lawless debut. He plummeted into language like an avalanche, as if it were his one escape route from death – which, of course, it was. He had been locked for years in the coffin of his body, unable to utter. When he found words he played rapturously with them, making them riot and lark about, echoing, alliterating and falling over one another. The bulging vocabulary kept sending you to the dictionary ('lassistral'? 'lemberyinth'?), only to find, more often than not, that you were far beyond charted usage, floundering fathomless in Nolan's neological sea.

It was, of course, a tragic book too. But the tragedy was challenged (as in this book) by the resourcefulness of the very language which expressed it. Nolan constantly subverted and remade idiom. He wrote, for instance, of tears that 'peter down my face', reminding us of the idiom 'peter out', which we use of paths that go nowhere or speech that dies away, but pushing the idiom askew, so that we see these new tears – slow, silent, hopeless – as we have never quite seen tears before.

The energy, newness and abundance of *Dam-Burst* can be found in this book too. Joseph's nightly dreams, for example, become ethereal and lexical forays – 'mesmerized woldwaddling in inkblue heaven's busy mobility of secrets'. The linguistic puzzles persist as well. Certain words – 'fees', 'fresco' – have, you come to realize, special meanings for Nolan, and understanding this unties some

ix

knots. 'Frescoed delights' at the Dún an Óir dance, and 'he frescoed farsighted fame' (in the Co. Clare shore scene) both suggest something bright, larger than life, and (like a fresco) seen but not shared in. The meaning is not too hard to catch.

But how about (to choose one example from scores) Joseph's realization that he can never marry: 'he had long ago snapped shut his challenging, fees-fashioned future and humanhinded his woldway as a celibate pilgrim through life'? 'Fees-fashioned', given Nolan's use of 'fees' to mean 'sacrifice', is manageable. But 'humanhinded'? It is deceptively like, and bitterly unlike, 'humankinded': but what does it mean? Is the 'hind' element 'hind' as in 'behindhand', or as in 'hindrance', or as in 'hind' (simple country fellow)? Or all three? This sense of language expanding beyond its own boundaries, and beyond our reach, is a typical Nolan effect, and one thing that prompts the frequently made comparison with Joyce.

Despite these similarities with the previous book, *Under the Eye of the Clock* is different, and a development. Plain statement and straightforward reportage now intermix with the bravura passages, allowing Nolan new kinds of tonal contrast, a new capacity for extended narrative, and a new realism. The observed world takes on unaccustomed clarity by courtesy of his verbal skills. On a beach, he watches the 'soft greased waves' creep towards him; horses in the market square release their 'musty urine' and: 'in artistic fashion it scribbled away breaking here and there into little rivulets all chasing after their pitiful bend'. Compare this with the tears that petered down his face in *Dam-Burst* and you can see that the vision has now been turned outward. The imaginative response is as acute, but a self-forgetting empathy now embraces the observed world – even its horse urine. The showpiece of this kind of creativity is the description of Joseph's mother gutting a turkey – a passage which should find its way into future anthologies of English prose. Like much of Nolan's writing, it combines a child's weird fanciful sympathy ('A huge gllomp sighed from the depths within') with the mind and vocabulary of an adult.

This double act is something Nolan clearly recognizes in

himself, and identifies as a fruit of his disability. It was because he realized the terrible truth about his body that, he relates, when only three years old, 'he cried the tears of a sad man'. *Dam-Burst* already showed a brilliant ironic acuteness in describing other people's reaction to his crippledom, and the same unsentimental intelligence appeared in the poems he wrote about his parents. Mature and considerate, they seemed to be written by a grown-up looking back, not by a child. He spoke of his paralysis as if it were some piece of adult news which he had, regretfully, to break to innocent bystanders: 'Woefully once I totally opened their eyes'. Similarly, in the poem 'Dad and Mam', the sophisticated diction used throughout contrasts calculatedly with the 'Dad' and 'Mam' in the title, so that those juvenile forms of address seem to be recalled from some much earlier stage of life.

In *Under the Eye of the Clock* this strangely poised detachment from himself and his condition – a detachment which is still hopelessly trapped in the disabilities it frees itself from – continues to intrigue the reader and, it seems, the writer too. He dreams he is a window-cleaner, balanced on a 'rattly silver ladder', cleaning big circles with his plaid cloth – whistling, active, happy – when suddenly, through the glass, he catches sight of a boy asleep in a bed – himself. The question this dream prompts, 'how can Boyhood be in two places at the same time?' – is what the whole book, with its extraordinary alliance of distance and closeness, answers.

Another area where this book shows both continuity and advance is the religious. The writer's Catholicism was already firm and clear in *Dam-Burst*. But the reader felt uneasy about its very firmness and clarity. Was not faith too pat a consolation, in the circumstances? How could it endure such a pitiless doom? How can you forgive a God who has put you into a spastic's body? Maybe these questions occur more readily to readers who are not Catholics, but at all events the poems did not answer them, nor did they do more than hint at the furious outcries and reproaches with which this ruined boy arraigned his Maker. *Under the Eye of the Clock* confronts this problem, so that we see more clearly what faith is. In one of the book's most dramatic scenes,

Joseph has himself wheeled up to the great crucifix in St John the Baptist's in order to swing his arm in a grand defiant arc and raise two fingers to the hanging Christ. The blasphemy is followed by a sense of absurdity: 'Imagine telling God to fuck off'. But this thought does not come as repentance. It is Hell, Joseph believes, that whispers it to him, laughing at his futility. The faith which in the poems was safety and strength becomes a battlefield.

For a preface which did not need writing in the first place, this has gone on long enough. But there is one thing to add. It would be possible to praise and analyse Nolan's book as one would the work of any brilliantly gifted young writer, without reference to his physical condition. That might, indeed, appear the tactful and seemly procedure. It would, however, be misguided in my opinion. The point is not that one has to make 'allowances'. Nolan's disability is not a handicap which has to be charitably offset against failures in accomplishment. Rather, it is a positive factor which adds immensely to the book's value and significance. For this is a voice coming from silence, and a silence that has, as Nolan is aware, lasted for centuries. He has a keen sense of the generations of mute, helpless cripples who have been 'dashed, branded and treated as dross', for want of a voice to tell us what it feels like. Now that voice – or at any rate that redeeming link with a typewriter – has come, and we know. On page after page of this book, Nolan tells us. It should not be possible, after reading it, ever again to think as we have before about those who suffer what he suffers. That is what makes it not just an outstanding book but a necessary one.

JOHN CAREY

CHAPTER ONE

A MODICUM OF ALOE

C AN you credit all of the fuss that was made of a cripple, mused Joseph Meehan as he settled his back against the seat for the flight home to Dublin. Now he had gained enough confidence to ask Nora to order a cup of coffee for him. Heretofore he had always declined any offer of refreshments, fearful always of creating a scene if fluid swallowed awkwardly went against his breath. 'Tea or coffee?' enquired the Aer Lingus hostess. 'Coffee, two coffees please,' said Nora. It came as a surprise to Nora when Joseph indicated in his silent code that he was bold enough now to attempt the arduous feat for him of swallowing down something in public. As his mother sensed his new-found bravery, she determined to pour small slurps of the coffee into his nervous mouth. Determinedly he smuggled the beverage past his decidedly stubborn tongue and let it seep down into his stomach. Snuggling his head then against the seat he slyly slipped away from Nora and scrambled silk blessings from cotton-wool casts.

'Hey, wake up,' said Nora as she nudged him with her elbow. 'Look down, there's Ireland's Eye,' she said, and glancing down he saw the beautiful coast of his country etching a welcome to a man in boy's garb.

Tanned by glory, Joseph was met at the airport by his father Matthew Meehan and his sister Yvonne. Bread given by Britain secreted juniper juice from spastic lonesomeness. Since sealing his fame as a special prizewinner by fashionably flying to London to receive his literary award, he now was even more heartened when Yvonne showed him the cutting from the daily newspaper describing the presentation under the headline 'Spastic Irish Boy Honoured'. Casting his mind back to London, Joseph again sampled the wonderful experience he gained by meeting with the enlightened members of the British Spastics Society. They amazed him by their understanding and by the dignity with which they dealt with him. Their breadth of vision mesmerized him and their sureness comforted his hassled world.

Newspapers bombarded constantly, each one eager to be first with the story of how a cripple came to vie with able-bodied man, especially in the area of wanton frankness as applied to literature and its brash experts. Joseph Meehan sat and listened as Nora mastered the responsibility of dealing with avid journalists, researchers for radio and television and newly interested script-writers. What am I garnering from all this jousting attention, pondered the alert boy. Casting glances of concern towards his family he noted the affront to their privacy, the yes associated with their handling of his hassle-filled, nodding-headed, creative though silent communication. He sadly fought to make his heart-felt plea – don't let the media create a monster out of me.

Sad thoughts destroy feasible mind's creation, so Joseph decided to flow with the current, minding each rapid as best he could. Assessing his progress to date occupied his night-time reverie:

> well OK
> what have I accomplished thus far
> fashioned you mean
> fashioned?
> damn you didn't I stay alive
> when all thought I was dead
> same difference
> same lottery
> gaseous life
> dastardly hemmed in
> in fools parade
> lonely freshness
> don't dare breathe
> thread up and spin again

frock bright
new material
moths nil
voce void
bone lambasted
joisted joyness
hall of fame
rank clichés
omens nod
put time off
random notes
past renegade boys
brengun farted
lonesomeness nigh volumes
offended newt
nodded echoed love light
through cactus-dry solent
in secluded concern.

Sons of bitches put on the casing of sobriety to gratify their mentors, but Joseph Meehan enriched himself by exhibiting his drunken, drooling body for all to see. Century upon century saw crass crippled man dashed, branded and treated as dross in a world offended by their appearance, and cracked asunder in their belittlement by having to resemble venial human specimens offering nothing and pondering less in their life of mindless normality. So Joseph mulled universal moods as he grimly looked back on the past, but reasons never curb but rather create new gleeful designs.

Access to the normal man's world came through Joseph's break-through to written creative musing. He had honestly yearned for a means of communication, but time goaded him as year followed year and he cradling still his mystical assessments and his nemesis-casted notions.

Seers cannot annoy themselves with masking looks, but cunning man mocking vocalic-seeming signs from brash brain-damaged brothers sifted certain secret solace from watching squirming casted embarrassingly within Joseph's handicapped boyhood. But new momentous pondering was in fact greengrass growing in Joseph Meehan's land. Wasting no time, he breathed his bona-fide beliefs; poetry was his vehicle of expression and truth his hallmark. Best assessed messages lighted his writing, trying as he was to solve the mystery surrounding spoilt manhood, birthed brain-damaged, but curiously, though seldom recognized, intellectually normal. Leaning on his family he cast down the gauntlet – accept me for what I am and I'll accept you for what you're accepted as.

And so the battle was staged between a crippled, sane boy and a hostile, sane, secretly savage though sometimes merciful world.

Can I climb man-made mountains, questioned Joseph Meehan. Can I climb socially constructed barriers? Can I ask my family to back me when I know something more than they, I now know the heinous scepticism so kneaded down constantly in my busy sad world. What can a crippled, speechless boy do, asked Joseph, my handicap curtails my collective conscience, obliterates my voice, beckons ridicule of my smile and damns my chances of being accepted as normal.

Joseph lay in his night sampan. As usual sleep nodded, but conscience never allowed rest to negate its nightly questioning. How do I overcome my muteness, he pondered. He nested a cassabled frankness, but felt he must find a way to communicate with boys and girls of his own age and who belonged to that great able-bodied world. He tossed and turned his mental giants and followed trains old and new, he asked for destinations man never knew existed. He boldly charged his driver – take me to no-man's land so that I can snare man as he wanders muted by loneliness. Had he but known man's memory never seems to cap its can but rather hovers kestrel-like, wings outspread, beady-eyed for any scent of despair, when swiftly it nosedives doleful buccaneers of venom to break the lonely flayed osprey, man's pent-up hurts. Casts of worms mark Dollymount Strand but casts of conscience lay on Joseph's pillow. He now knew his appointed route and must manoeuvre fabulous destination a few steps nearer every day, otherwise he failed in his concordat with cranks.

Able only to sit in his wheelchair, Joseph always depended on others to propel his chair for him. Family members were safe and sure but he also had his friend Alex Clark, and Alex devoted time and trouble to not only pushing Joseph's wheelchair, but to being one of Joseph's acute and early friends. Alex's friendship dated back to the young boy's schooldays at the national school attached to Dublin's Central Remedial Clinic. Girls and boys disabled by some form of handicap shared Joseph's early years in the clinic. Only slightly physically handicapped, Alex brought his strength into play and sacking Joseph's cross of much of its sting, he helped his friend to sample some of the good things of life. Together the two boys went to the local shop; together they played football, Alex pushing the wheelchair, football nestling between the wheels as nearing the goal, Alex then kicked and both boys shared the scored goal. When nobody was watching the pair became Jackie Stewarts. They raced along the corridors, Alex standing upon the shafts of the chair while at the same time steering it.

Each jaunt brought greater daredevil status, and besting teacher's eagle eyes became a daily challenge. But a day of reckoning dawned. The coast proved clear, the pair set off at top speed but neither took account of the desk newly placed outside a classroom door. Speeding along, the small front wheel of Joseph's chair glanced off the leg of the desk. Sudden can be the only word to describe Joseph's ejection from his breathtaking seat. Like a cannonball he shot from his chair, up in the air he flew and down he crashed on his forehead. Dizzy designs displayed upside-down corridor, consciousness marked frantic footsteps, voices wavered and waned, but in a few moments view cleared and Joseph felt himself being lifted back into his seat. Nurse Brown rushed him to her screened room and quickly she placed an icepack on his head. Alex was scared stiff and Joseph was scared sober for what would happen when Nora came to collect him. Nothing happened, because parents realize that boys have got to be boys despite being disabled.

Boyhood friendships say a lot for future dreams but before the future makes inroads, dear friends establish grand links that time or place cannot scuttle. Alex gave of himself and great gladness became beautiful though distance was eventually to separate the two friends. Forgetting never, Joseph scanned often the greatness of their comradeship. As usual he captured again the security felt when a mute crippled boy has a brave vocal friend. He remembered anew the famous concert. Alex became ill with flu and so Joseph found himself forgotten. Belgrove Boy's School Band were coming to give a recital in the CRC School. All pupils were invited. Each classroom emptied as children followed teacher to the all-purposes room. As Alex was absent nobody thought of bringing Joseph. He sat forgotten in his classroom. As the music started up he strained his ears to hear it. He secretly became dunce in the corner facing the wall. As he grew tired of that pose he became Miss Ryan teaching about faith in God and faith in your fellow man. Glancing around the classroom, his eye fell on the map of Europe, and Ireland's newest captain piloted his kinky plane down the runway prior to taking off for never-never land. The music still gushed in the distance, the tune was Molly Malone:

> 'In Dublin's fair city,
> Where the girls are so pretty,
> I first set my eyes on sweet Molly Malone,
> As she wheeled her wheelbarrow,
> Through streets broad and narrow,
> Crying, 'Cockles and mussels,
> Alive, alive O!'

Casting himself as John McCormack, the great Irish tenor, Joseph swelled his chest, stiffened his neck and began to roar out his volcanic version of Molly Malone. He resurrected a singer from the grave, sang forced sound but music not at all. Must Ireland's newest tenor clap himself on the back he chortled, but peddling his feet on the metal footrest of his chair he coughed and made ready for his next game. Seeing youth in all its colours he now saw his version of Van Gogh take shape. He looked at the pupils' paintings all around the classroom and he replaced them with a self-portrait, ear missing, no bandage, chambers of the ear gaping open, fiercely listening. As he caught the mood of the moment he replaced golden yellow with threatening gun-metal grey. What'll I do next he pondered. Never minding his aloneness he cast his gaze in the direction of Belgrove Girl's School. Abutting his own one-man concert he now dubbed his lonely mystifying boyhood with favourite lemon-listless sweeteners. He thought of his no longer free sister as she sat in a three-storeyed school. Hers must be the loss when she had to come to the city of his new-found freedom. There he could imagine her as she sat in a huge class. He suddenly burst out laughing for now he was as juggler in his fractured domain. He sat giggling to the echoed stillness. He cast bossy man aside and accompanied his sister through her staged one-girl-show. She, nimble of wit, could never understand how folk failed to capture the mind hinting from her brother's eyes. Thus it was that she stood in for restless, mindless man and single-handedly she scaped weasel-grasp of her brother's life, thereby cresting normality where ignorance crested scary fear.

Creaking his neck he again looked up at the first landing on the stairs at home. She stood there and in dramatic fashion she recited school-told poems. James Weldon Johnson's 'clickin' together of the dry bones, dry bones' suggested negro-voiced thinking. Now her mind turned and Hilaire Belloc's 'Tarantella' danced 'Out and in' through his memory. Yvonne brengun-blasted his silence as he sat in his wheelchair looking up towards her on the landing stage. She switched on and off the sly two way switch leaving him in semi-darkness while the top landing light managed to give her sufficient credibility before her Sesame-like appearance. She sometimes looked over the top landing banister to watch his reaction after a number for now the stream of light was on the audience. He grinned and chortled begging for more. She hurriedly changed costumes and switching back the light appeared again to dance hearty jigs and reels to her own lilted accompaniment. Now it was time for music so peering up against the light he saw Yvonne put her mouth to the tin whistle and he was haunted by her 'Danny Boy', 'Roddy McCorley', 'My Lagan Love' and 'It's A Long Way To Tipperary'. Nine years old he was but his was the joy of a man and all because of an eleven year old girl's imagination. But her show held one final number. Queer swishing swirled about as she dressed herself for it. Rustling skirts hinted of frills and flounces. Suddenly she let out wild cheers and switching back the light she hurried down the steps to her landing and there before him he saw the Folies Bergère take shape as she danced and high kicked a cancan to her own breathless la la-ing. Closing her dance sequence she threw herself down in a final split, her frilled underskirts standing like a peacock's tail over her bold head. She was exhausted but he was enthralled. The doors to the hall had been locked, her one-girl show was for him alone. Truly her freshness grew green lily leaves on his stagnant pond.

Mental games ceased abruptly when he heard the opening chord of the National Anthem. Oh! here they come thought Joseph, I must not appear sad, anyway I'm not. But he knew that Miss Ryan would be feeling secretly sorry for him so he charged himself to convince her that he was happy. Getting his smile ready he waited. Yells of excitement poured into the corridor, voices varied and then the door opened: 'Ah God, look at poor Joseph,' they cried in unison. Miss Ryan had heard their cry and coming through the door she seemed to cringe with hurt for doleful boyhood, forgotten by all, and dimpled he smiled a happy smile especially meant to comfort her hurt.

Pupils in the Central Remedial Clinic School were always nestled in a caring collective society. Each student exhibited some form of handicap: some had serious disablement while others were only slightly affected. Joseph sat among his classmates but his handicap was scurrilously fret-filled. He was castrated by crippling disease, molested by scathing mockery, silenced by paralysed vocal muscles yet ironically blessed with a sense of physical well-being. He felt cheated though, for his healthy feeling seemed to vex his limbs into rebellion. The frenzied limbs could wreak involuntary havoc yet he was unable to even brush a fly off his nose. Sampling school life he sat each day eking out and living a normal life among pupils, who for some self-adorning reason, delineated sense to what they themselves spoke, but donned gabbled lost meaning to the sentences which Joseph, nested in hassled lucidity, served up in boyish hesitance and leased forever from heliotrope ages of Hell.

Cheering each aspect of fun created comedy for all the class. Children sampled homespun humour at Joseph's expense; accordingly Joseph too acquired some benefit from seeming a fool in other people's eyes. He was only tasking them to assess his language, but at the same time he was measuring their youthful lack of imagination as sometimes he expressed hididdledee while they suggested meanings sadly containing some of their own hurt feelings. Joseph washed himself free of their wish to hurt his feelings and instead developed a spine of iron coupled with a volcanic wish to become more adept at communicating his beliefs and certainties.

Making fun for the class became the custom and on this particular day handsome Eamonn Cambell donned the comic's robe. He let the air out of the tyres of the two wheels of Joseph's wheelchair. Then he defied Joseph to be able to tell the teacher. Miss Ryan entered the classroom after coffee-break and determined not to fail, Joseph set about making his complaint. He peddled furiously on the footrest of his chair in order to catch her attention. She glanced down at Joseph. He peddled more furiously building up to a great crescendo while at the same time keeping a wary eye on her face. She frowned and then an enquiring look lit up her face. Joseph then caught her gaze and with his eyes drew her sight downwards to his flat-rimmed wheel. He repeated his sweeping eye course until she walked down to stand before him and to look closely into his eyes. He drew her eyes downwards to his wheels. 'What's wrong Joseph, is something wrong with your chair?' she asked. He nodded his offended nod and she glanced hard at his wheel. 'Oh you've got a puncture,' she said. Joseph looked into her face and swung her gaze to the other wheel. Keeping his head turned towards the other wheel she walked around to the other side of his chair. 'Oh, someone let the air out of your wheels,' she observed. 'Who did that?' she demanded, but Joseph jumped into action and nodded accusingly at Eamonn. Eamonn denied having had anything to do with Joseph's wheelchair. 'Right,' said Miss Ryan, 'we'll have a trial by jury. A courtroom hearing we'll have, and I'll be the judge.' The hearing got underway; the plaintiff was Joseph, the defendant was Eamonn; eyewitnesses were called to give evidence and the rigged jury were unable to give a unanimous verdict, so a split decision was sure to please both sides. The judge then rapped out her attention to order and with a gleam in her eye she quashed the sitting and asked the accuser and the accused to shake hands. Eamonn walked swiftly to Joseph's side and bending down he grasped his accuser's hand and shook it warmly. Then turning to Miss Ryan he suggested that he'd go in search of a pump to inflate the flat tyres for Joseph. From that day forward Eamonn claimed Joseph among his normal friends.

Teachers make or mar the confidence of their pupils. In Joseph's case his teachers made his confidence strong by not alone deciphering his coded communication, but by being imaginative enough to help him to share the experiences of children who were only slightly disabled. They helped him play pingpong and the fact that the ball did not hit the table but flew out the window did not stop Mr O'Mahony from holding firm to Joseph's hand, and together they strived to do better with their next grand stroke.

Assorted and thrilling treats were possible because teachers brought them within Joseph's sphere. Through his teachers he met the famous Canadian Mounties, the newly crowned All-Ireland football champions, the Dublin team nicknamed Heffo's Army, and he was even let size up their great trophy, the Sam Maguire Cup, at close range.

The teachers sometimes had to bear the brunt of handicap by physically carrying their pupils, and so concerned were they that they kindled great spirits in their handicapped charges. An open-topped, double-decked bus visited the school. Seeing a doleful longing in Joseph's eyes, Paul O'Mahony carried the crippled boy up the steep stairs and sitting him on his lap, he brought him on the bus tour of Clontarf. The voice of the teacher nulled fate's abuses as man to man he pointed out the historic and mundane aspects of this ancient region. Such were Paul O'Mahony's attitudes to dealing with disabled students that he decided to bring the kitchen into the classroom. 'We'll cook Irish Stew tomorrow' he said and there and then he set about calling out the ingredients. On the morrow together with his pupils he cooked the stew.

Senses dormant sprung into being as the broth gave off the savoury smell one associates with kitchen, apron territory.

Such were Joseph's teachers and such was their imagination that the mute boy became constantly amazed at the almost telepathic degree of certainty with which they read his facial expression, eye movements and body language. Many a good laugh was had by teacher and pupil as they deciphered his code. It was at moments such as these that Joseph recognized the face of God in human form. It glimmered in their kindness to him, it glowed in their keenness, it hinted in their caring, indeed it caressed in their gaze.

Clontarf got its name from the gaelic Cluain Tarbh (the meadow of the bull), and the origin of the title was historically recorded as the bellowing sound of the sea as it cavernously roared its angry way down and up over the vast sandbanks of the bay of Dublin. But Clontarf had called glory towards itself in a more definite way when King Brian Boru defeated the Vikings in the great Good Friday Battle of Clontarf in 1014. Joseph was familiar with the folklore of ancient Clontarf, but fuel was added to imagination's fire when he came to live in this north Dublin suburb. Many a summer evening he was to witness battles fought out by Irishmen in similar spirit to Brian Boru, but all in the cause of team glory and magical entertainment. His father was his constant companion at the football matches in St Anne's Park and he kicked every kick of the ball with his bold son. Wintertime saw them both at the great rugby workouts in Castle Avenue grounds. Oftentimes they watched the international rugby squad doing their pre-match runs and passes. But that was the world of the able-bodied; poor Joseph was only a looker-on. More and more though he longed to rub shoulders with the young able-bodied people, but keeping in mind his difficulties he feared for his chances.

Frowning with concentration, Joseph cackled with determination as he collected his brambles of boyhood's success. Disabled schemes met with beautiful basting in the Central Remedial Clinic, but now he scanned burly boys and loneliness crept nearer as he watched students spill home from the local schools and colleges. His capability to adjust to dealing with able-bodied classes outside of the shelter of the CRC School assumed a numbing importance in his youthful scheme of things. Can I do it, he wondered during long dark hours as he lay curled up in his bed. Are crepuscular dreams really the stuff of normality, worried Joseph, or cod's claims caught wanting in the cold grey light of dawn. Queer questioning answered his dark dreams. Much foolhardy frankness mesmerized his mind. Who'll have you, who'd be fool enough – maybe you're biting off more than you can chew – chew damnblast chew, if I could chew I could call myself normal, imagine, can't chew, can't swallow, so why chew? can't call – can call, a famished moan maybe yet it suffices; can't chew, can't chew, can't smell – can smell – can't chew, can't control bowels – can, can, can control, can't control bladder – can control, can control; can't chew though so what, I have a dry seat, lovely dry seat, always, always, but can't chew, can't cry – can cry, can cry, can cry wet pillows full but who cares, can cry, cry bucketfuls, can't laugh – can laugh, can, can, can, can't stop – can stop, can't see why I should, can't see why, can't see the need, can't blame me, help say something sad: Can't Chew.

Credited with an above average intelligence, he now sought a school masterful enough to accept a silent cripple on their rollcall of normal, perfect-featured boys and girls. Ranted refusals sacked Joseph's lovely glad life of messaged massiveness when he heard his parents accept that assessed, crippled boyhood could not be hors d'oeuvred on the menu of a normal, flashy school. Dear oh dear, what would parents think if they saw a cripple in the same cast as their darlings, chorused Joseph's fears as he desperately listened to Nora speaking on the telephone to a headmaster of a local comprehensive school. 'I'm prepared to have him,' said the headmaster, 'but someone always vetoes his application whenever his name comes up for consideration at our board meetings.' Someone always vetoes his application thought Joseph, and his mind addressed the treasured sanctum of a board meeting: someone always vetoes; someone normal; someone beautiful; someone blessed by normality; someone administering the rusty mind's rules of yesteryear; someone male – cigar-smoker perhaps; someone ruddy-faced with health; someone female – a skeleton in her cupboard, never give a sucker an even break; someone Christian worst of all, boasted ascetic, one of the head-strokers – poor child, God love him, ah God is good, never shuts one door but he opens another; someone genuine not able to bend the rules to match the need; someone satanic revelling in the sufferings of others; someone versed in the art of saying no; someone who had too many nos in their childhood; someone able to say no to a dumb cripple; someone always says no.

Writhing from the sting of rejection and smelling the wax from his melted wings he erstwhile assumed a wait-and-see attitude. Advising himself not ever to look back, he joyfully mulled a new blood-red wine with a modicum of aloe.

Crestfallen but not frantic, Matthew Meehan hurt for his son's sake. Never one to keep silent whilst the sensitivity of another was being trampled upon, he described how brash man had vetoed Joseph's admission to a local school. He accounted his story to a fellow member of staff at work, psychiatrist Dr Brian McCaffrey. The doctor listened intently and he then expressed the wish to meet Joseph.

The front door opened at lunch hour that day and Matthew could be heard chatting with somebody as he showed them into the lounge. Matthew called Nora and Joseph and introduced them both to Dr McCaffrey. Joseph brashly conversed in his own language, leaving no doubt in the doctor's mind that here was a boy ready and willing to face school life bravely if only a school would have him. Dr McCaffrey got the vibes better than most newcomers and looking at Joseph he said, 'I'd like to help you and I think I can. Can I use your telephone?' he enquired of Matthew, and together they went towards the hall. Following a brief conversation, Dr McCaffrey returned to the lounge and looking Joseph straight in the eye he voiced something that Joseph longed to hear. 'Listen, Joseph, you are to go for an interview to Mount Temple School. Now take it from me they'll judge you on your merits. They never had a handicapped pupil before but they would like to meet you.' Schooling himself to fiercely thank this great-hearted human being Joseph asked Nora to fetch his typewriter and sincerely he typed, 'You are very humble to care about me.' Then catching Dr McCaffrey's eye, he drew his gaze towards the typewritten message. He watched for a response and was cheered by the tear which he saw glistening in this caring man's eye. 'You're very deserving of my help,' he said, 'and I'm glad to have been able to introduce you. Now, Joseph, the rest is up to you.' Indeed the rest *was* up to Joseph and casting his bent shoulder to the wheel of fobbed-off fortune, he fathomed deep worries as he looked towards interview day.

CHAPTER TWO

HELL GUFFAWED

JOSEPH Meehan leapt awake that morning. Crawling with nerves he cried out, 'Lord above, I've to go for that bloody interview today.' Then he cringed in fear. Slob that he was, he knew now before the day was out he'd have cooked his goose for good and all. He lay in his bed frightening himself and then relaxing himself. Wait till the headmaster sees you doing your war dance he teased himself, but right away he countered: maybe you won't be nervous at all, maybe you'll be grand and relaxed, you know it happens sometimes, remember the first time you ever received communion, that day you were as calm as the desert after a sandstorm. Vests of vanquished heaven bucked his boy's god-given loneliness but at the same time hell guffawed in loud mocking laughs.

Creaking with nerves he sat in his chair. His parents were preparing to take their zoo-caged son to meet John Medlycott, the headmaster of Mount Temple Comprehensive School. Don't worry, he whispered to himself, be brave, rest awhile. Desperate in the face of crying God's fear he waited to go on youthful trial. Plodding bravery abandoned him, Joseph Meehan now joined hushed criminals before the firing squad.

Matthew reversed the car out onto the road and switching on the radio he pretended that all was normal but his eye seemed to glance too often towards his son. Nora meanwhile supported her son's frame with her arm. He hugged her closer to his frail body as if he could draw strength from her courage. As the car eased into the gateway he glanced ahead at the spired school. A large clock face warned him that it had seen history recorded, but numb now he baulked before its long-handed beckoning. Matthew lifted him from his seat and placed him in his lonely chair. Then together parents and boy set off to find the principal's office.

Bidden to come in, the crippled wheelchair-bound boy braved it across the threshold of the headmaster's office. Seated at a desk he saw a bright-eyed, bearded man. What the headmaster saw could barely be believed, for, true to form, arms spread wide open, face suddenly locked tight in an expression of stupid-looking languor, Joseph Meehan made his grand entrance. The first attempt to smile at Mr Medlycott's welcoming words sent Joseph's body into spasm making facial muscles contort and making his arms and legs move violently just as a clock-work doll would move on being released to unwind. The poor headmaster must have been bewildered by what he faced, but Nora mastered his bafflement by candidly saying, 'As you can see Joseph is very nervous but he'll relax in a few minutes.' Fashioning a faith which was totally against his better instincts, Mr John Medlycott smiled convincingly and waved aside any need for further explanation. Just then a tall bearded man stepped into the office. The principal introduced him as Jack Heaslip, the guidance counsellor. By this time Joseph had assumed a more relaxed state so he was able to pay attention to the teachers. Seconds passed into minutes and now Joseph was on the alert, storing away words and observations when suddenly the bombshell burst, bursting asunder all man's renegade constraints in dealing with disabled man. Gloriously grinning faith Mr Medlycott said, 'Well Joseph, when can you start?' Joseph acknowledged his question by assuming the stance of one about to levitate. He felt a surge of happiness rush through his heart, it melted all over his many rejections and schooled his resolve not ever to fail this warm-hearted schoolmaster. As if to establish a certainty in Joseph's mind Mr Medlycott picked up the house phone and said, 'Jim, would you come here for a moment?' The door opened again and brusquely a man breezed in. He was dressed in a thick-knit sweater and jeans and his deep copper coloured hair and beard seemed as if it was going to choke him. Joseph noticed not just the beard and smart haircut but creeping curls of red chest hair peeped up from inside his open-necked shirt. 'Mr Casey,' said the headmaster, 'I'd like you to meet Joseph Meehan', and turning to Joseph he said, 'Joseph, meet Mr Casey, he'll be your class tutor.' Mr Casey smiled and said, 'Welcome, Joseph, to this school', and turning he shook hands with Matthew and Nora. Then feeling for the youngster's excitement he said, 'Come on Joseph, I'll bring you on a tour of the school', and off they set, the friendly striding teacher and the wheelchair-bound, silent, though thinking boy.

Silence reigned in the corridors, murmurs could be heard in the classrooms as Jim Casey pushed him along. The teacher showed him the library, the art room, the dining hall and then taking his bunch of keys from his pocket, he opened the door of his own classroom. He eased the chair into the crowded room. Empty desks stood in packed rows, a big blackboard lined the wall, but it was the windows that caught Joseph's attention. They were placed up near the ceiling and Joseph wondered why so high, why get only a glimpse of the sky. Feeling for the young boy's curiosity, Jim Casey asked and answered questions that he felt might be racing through Joseph's mind. The boy was flummoxed by the teacher's imagination and as he listened he hurrahed silently, for Mount Temple was going to answer his dreams. Lighting flickered for a moment when Jim Casey switched it off, and then locking the door again the teacher and boy set about returning to the office. Between them the teachers decided then to introduce Joseph to two boys who would be classmates of his. Mr Medlycott had chosen them and asked them to help Joseph to fit in to life in Class 1L. The boys seemed nervous and ill-at-ease, but the contact had been made and each boy had now got time to think and adjust to their coming challenge. Joseph asked nothing but verily quaked at what was before him. As usual though, he heaved a prayer and manfully faced his future in Mount Temple Comprehensive School. Now it was time to go and Joseph dearly wished to thank the teachers, but even so spasms ruled out obvious vests of gratitude and instead grimaces, gutteral sounds and dancing foot movements were all that he could muster up. Hesitating on the threshold he made one last effort to express thanks. Steadying his head he looked Mr Medly-cott straight in the eye and gave a series of staccato-rapid bows. John Medlycott was not found wanting and Joseph smiled naturally for the first time that day, but there would be other days, that he knew full well, for wasn't every opportunity about to be dragged forth to birth new light into his drab-dreamed world.

Accommodating Joseph's fears was Nora's job, and she sensed that sealed within him was a beautiful brittle sensitivity. She knew that he was disappointed with his personal showing in Mount Temple but on the drive home she chatted to Matthew about the size of the school, the great acreage of grounds, the obvious sports facilities and the awareness of the three teachers whom she had just met. Clearly declining any effort on Joseph's part to talk about restoring confidence after his highly cantankerous-looking display, Nora waited until they all arrived home. Then stretching reliable allowances she looked at Joseph and said, 'Well Joseph, how does it feel to have all that fuss behind you?' All his silent, pent-up despair burst wide open and poor Joseph cried out loud, forgetting the adage that big boys don't cry, very sure they must if life hellishly harasses them, and not giving a damn whether they did or not, he cried fullsome tears of thoughtful, shattered, bewildering bewilderment. How must I have looked to those sane men? How can I convince them of my sanity? Were they really shattered in the face of my mad body antics? Were they only extending the typical hand of Protestant Christian concern or were they as damnwell terrified of me as I was of facing them? And next time we meet I have to be geared to face eight hundred students as well. Yesteryear's tears certainly were the stuff of childhood but now today's tears were for bewildering now and castrated boy's future.

Feebly, Nora and Matthew tried to divine the depths of their sad son's despair but bravely they hotly confirmed his own summing-up. 'Yes,' said Matthew, 'you were tense, but what you don't realize is that those teachers were equally tense, but they could hide it. Better for them to see you at your worst, things can only get better for you and for them.' Nora, usually sympathetic, destroyed Joseph's scene by gleefully laughing at him. Never heeding his therapeutic tears she said, 'Come boy, you know you have made the first scrape on the canvas, wait and see what's in store.' Punching Joseph in the chest then she smilingly sauntered off to cook the dinner.

But nobody can choke back such salty tears, so Joseph continued snivelling for some time. He knew his parents slyly meant to shock him into manhood, but he was not going to give in just yet.

At dinner that evening Nora denounced her son for being a coward. 'Come on Joseph, don't be so damn dramatic,' she begged. 'Didn't you meet your teachers and two pupils, and didn't you get the feel of the school? Now be man enough to give yourself and them a chance.' Joseph was still feeling hard done by but he knew his mother was sealing the day by challenging him to think positively. Even so, he struggled between hope and despair. Feeling tired from the huge task of meeting and convincing the uninitiated, he eventually gave in. Counselling himself not to weary himself any more he grew calm. As usual consolation came and as usual it was bonded in beautiful boldness. What trestled his mind bore no resemblance to sadness, for as usual, and unasked, hollow, nebulous, clinging clouds of heliotrope happiness came to rescue the broken resolution in this young boy's battle.

Dead weary, Joseph went to bed that night thankful that his day for introduction to Mount Temple was over. Dearly he thanked his Master for numbing his voiceless despair. He pictured in his mind the great-hearted men that he had just met and he knew that they anointed him by first fastening faith in a future which would include a handicapped boy on their rollcall. Sizing up his future he counselled himself to describe what the past endured and what the future might hold. Look at your lessons boy, he chivvied. Consider how lucky you are. You have served your time to coldness in outlook. Now you have got your foot in the door, maybe you ought to panic. Think of the others gone before you – did they have fiery intellects? Were they stored away in a back room, dirty, neglected, frowned upon? Did sun ever tan their opaque skin? Did they ever see the night sky? Did kindness ever move them to tears? Did they ever delve their hand in cold water? Did someone ever feel for their clenched fists and gently prise them open, so that water could run between their withered fingers? Did they feel the cold nervous heartbeat of a damp frog? Did they hold a wriggling worm in the palm of their hand? Did they ever feel soft summer rain as it tickled down their face or the headbowed battle to breathe in the face of a blizzard? Did they ever gloat with pleasure in a warm bubbly bath and afterwards sneeze in an aroma of talcum powder? Did sunshine blind them from an early-morning golden-copper sun, or did they ever see winter-bared trees silhouetted against crimson shot with pastel blue evening skies? Did they ever hear a real sound of laughter free of innuendo coming pouring from a pal's heart? Did they ever feel absolute satisfaction when the golf ball they were let help to hit rolled straight as a die and plopped into the minuscule-sized hole? Did they ever have their father's company on lovely secluded walks as birds did their nut, each bird bursting forth its chest trying to outdo its neighbour's song-filled stand? Did they ever feel a dear sister's love when she spent backbreaking hours designing and painting an intricate celtic drawing especially for them? Did they ever love a foolish dog and marvel at his happiness? Did they ever feel good omens? Did they ever heave a sigh of healthy feeling despite awful paralysis? Did they rush through breakfast to be in time for school? Did they wait for Santa unable to sleep, fretting that Santa wouldn't come if they were not asleep? Did they dare to carp if bad vibes came from their sister? Did they ever detect jealousy in their sister's clambering for bigger helpings, bigger toys, bigger slices of family attention? Did they ever get so much love that the able-bodied sister wished that she were crippled too? Did they ever? And if they didn't, was that the end of that? Nasty life cast a lonely shroud over their dreams, but years heard the silent cry of those bashful babes and cuteness cogitates years' findings. So, Joseph schooled his nerve, and so his resolve reverberated in the chambers of his soul.

Easing their car into the stream of morning traffic, Matthew and Nora filled in for voiceless Joseph. They wondered about the length of the day in school, about the subjects, wondered who would first befriend their son and wondered silently if he baulked inwardly. Joseph meanwhile sat and secretly fretted. He imagined what the pupils would be thinking when his voice would involuntarily ring out a screech associated with tension or what, he worried, will they think when my arms fly outstretched when they try pushing my wheelchair through the crowded corridors or, worst of all, will they think I'm bonkers if my hands suddenly fly forward and hit them in the face. As a gap developed in the traffic he felt the surge of speed as the car streamed forward bringing him ever quicker towards Mount Temple. Slowing down now, Matthew swung in to the gateway of his son's school. Sampling the thronged, frantic-running students, the boy gasped with fright. Cringing, he cowered beside his mother, but still his eye fell anew on the great clock facing him from the spired, sober-brick building.

Arriving at the front hall, Joseph found Peter Nicholson and Eddie Collins waiting for him. He searched their faces but saw only boyish civility and confidence. 'Can we bring you to your first class?' enquired Peter, but Matthew detained them, for he was anxious to explain about his son's involuntary arm movements. Nora said nothing; seemingly she was depending on the three boys to make up their own minds about how to deal with their new problems. 'I'll be here in this little office if you need me,' said Nora as she glanced towards a yellow door, and with that the boys and their new classmate set off down the corridor. Joseph was schooling his body to stay calm, whilst the boys were negotiating how they'd manage to curtail his arms. 'We are bringing you to the music room for singing,' confided Peter and there at the end of a green corridor they came upon a group of pupils standing waiting for the teacher to unlock the door. He let the boys and girls pass inside and then conscious of his new pupil, he came towards him and taking his hand he shook it warmly saying as he did so, 'You're very welcome to Mount Temple. I hope, Joseph, that you'll be very happy here with us.' Eddie then eased the wheelchair into the room and class began. Seeming curious, cheeky-faced Joseph moved his gaze from one student to the next whilst they, anxious not to seem afraid, quickly swerved away when his eye fell upon them. He smelt their utter fear of him but was anxious too not to add to their worry by getting tense and grimacing wildly as facial muscles twisted askew in spasm.

Prior to the end of class Peter and Eddie asked to be excused, explaining to the teacher that they needed a headstart in order to have the wheelchair delivered to the next class before the corridors became jammed with students careering in their hundreds at change of class. Casting around for something to talk about, Eddie and Peter faced their new charge and tried to include him in their conversation. All was going smoothly for the three boys, but nothing could have prepared them for what happened next. Suddenly the school siren blared bloody murder and, frightened out of his wits, his brain-damaged startle reflex gave an almighty leap frightening in turn poor Peter and Eddie half to death. Despite the fright the boys kept up a brave front. They recovered their confidence and asked Joseph if he was alright. Joseph grinned and silently cast his eyes towards the ceiling signalling yes.

Meeting Jim Casey the English teacher was next on the time-table. 'He's our class tutor, did you know that?' asked Peter as he wheeled Joseph into the English classroom. Glancing backwards into Peter's face, Joseph indicated yes. Smiling simple welcome, Mr Casey took the handles of the wheelchair and steered Joseph into a gap among the front row desks. Casting many a wary glance in Joseph's direction he commenced to teach his charges. School was taking on a new meaning for Joseph, and smartly he began to record his new insights. The silent boy watched and listened to Mr Casey's cradling of voiced moments in poetry, the likes of which he had never heard before. His method of recording was not very obvious, but with an acute and sensitive ear he listed and stored his findings. Mr Casey and his class were certain in their speech but their exchanges served his purpose for silently he too answered questions and waited then to see if anybody else shared his opinions.

Classes changed once again and history was the subject this time. 'We have the headmaster for history,' explained Peter as the three boys sauntered along. Silence in the corridors seemed to create a closeness between them and Joseph felt at ease in their company. The boys were first into the classroom and as the class members filed in Joseph sneaked sideways glances at them watching for fear to manifest itself, but more power to them, he found them reassuring in that they continued arguing, teasing and generally being their noisy selves. Mr Medlycott breezed in with a flourish as if to hint that yes he saw nothing unusual in his new class member. 'Now pay attention,' he said and determining where they were at in their history books he launched into his subject.

Breathing a sigh of relief, Joseph cast mental anguish aside as he and his charges headed up the corridor for the mid-morning break. Assessing pupils' attitudes towards him he feared the result. Poor-fashioned mannerisms plagued his appearance but he knew full well that great undertakings require great tender rescuers with great tender hearts, and young though he was he could feel the tenderness masked behind the seeming coldness of the teachers and now already some of the boys and girls in Class 1L.

As classes broke up for their fifteen-minutes' break, pupils eyed Joseph with great curiosity and bemusement. Peter and Eddie were by his side always, but childish-minded students classed both of them as gullible for wasn't it only too obvious that that boy was retarded.

Seeing the Irish teacher at the door of her classroom fencing a pathway in for the wheelchair made Joseph aware of something candid in the expression on the face of Miss Siney. She was dressed in grey but her eyes danced with friendliness. She spoke Irish as if her respect for it came not just from the fact that it was her native language, but that she relished the sound of pronunciation, in short she seemed to really love her mother tongue. Joseph caught Miss Siney's eye searching his face for a sign of interest in her subject, but all she saw was dull looks, dribbles and senseless sounds.

At five minutes to midday Peter and Eddie set off with their charge for Miss Craig's room for environmental studies. Breathing noisily from pure tension, Joseph steamed into the classroom. Voiceless, he could not convey his pleasure at meeting another new teacher, but Miss Craig beautifully bypassed the momentary embarrassment by carefully assisting the boys as they moved desks to make place for the wheelchair. Breathing quietly now, Joseph was able to size up his teacher. She emanated civil normal breadth of courage by creating an air of 'let there be no panic, I'm in control here,' and on she went with her geography lesson.

Cheering wildly in the corridors, all eight hundred students broke free for lunch hour. A smell of cooking wafted from the dining hall but Joseph verily cheered too, for his first day in Mount Temple was over and he was free to go home and cast rollicking fun for himself and his family by drolly giving a blow-by-blow account of the teachers, pupils, attitudes and foul-ups of his first great day in an able-bodied man's wonderful world.

Each day of that first week narrowed down to a half-day was cast especially to cater for Joseph's needs. The teachers felt that his introduction to school and pupils needed to be done gradually. So it was that he charged home that first day, and so it was that he had the second half of the day for conversation, waffle, frankness and even some wound-licking.

Dark night was always waned by golden visions and the night of 20 February 1979 was no different. Just as always happened, Joseph Meehan saw his life pass before his sensitive mind's eye. Free-falling, he created grand gospels of boyish certainty. Washed by sedentary, snared sacrifice he descended within easy reach of hell, but severe despondency never could stop Joseph's mesmerized woldwaddling in ink-blue heaven's busy mobility of secrets. Cassettes played back the day's happenings sadly beckoning him towards despair, but fending off fright he beckoned instead towards students frolicking in dreamland and stole yesses from them before they ebbed notional no.

CHAPTER THREE

WHITE SHEETS OF LIFE

MORNING yawned bright, and brimful with hyssop-hinted hope the young crippled boy faced his second day in his new school. As he drove by the one-eyed clock spire, he bowed in rescued boyhood for now he had faith in himself. He nymph-like looked respectfully towards his teachers and decided to give himself to them and to their students in 1L. Do with me what you can, he begged in whispered whimpering but, he fretted, I can be but my feeble self. Although he reasoned thus, yet he was full of hope for he had sensed security and kindness in Peter and Eddie's first attempts to communicate with him.

Joseph dreaded having to be a burden to his hyphenated school. 'Nisi Dominus Frustra' was their motto and plagued as he was, he believed boyish belief in a caring, thyme-scented, juxtaposing God. 'Except the Lord keep the city, the watchman waketh but in vain,' teased the school-momented psalm. Now the school was going to justify its beliefs by declaring that where God rests all are safe. Joseph felt his handicap in myriad ways but now he looked on and jumped with joy as he felt human hands helping to lift the cross ever so slightly from his shoulders. Ancient in origin, the modern Mount Temple (replacing old Mountjoy School) inculcated the psalm's teaching. The school was clustered at the feet of an imposing Victorian Gothic-designed house. Its spires expressed a foyered glance upwards whilst over the historic door still lingered the original script inscribed in 1862. The dedicated residents' ancient scroll nutshelled his belief *Via tentdanda est*, a way must be found. Now here Joseph Meehan sat in the twentieth century kindling anew the great spark within the protestant tradition of verved Christian brotherhood. He recognized their beliefs and they in turn recognized his.

In anchoring ship in Mount Temple, Joseph calmed foolish seas of vacant scanning, and cloyed bannered musings vacated his scolded, messaged notation. Austere casing wrapped him tightly, but fun, frolics and flutters marked out his future years' canvassed beat. He shrieked in fear now for dead dreams' recurrence but man-nosed frankness heeded Hecuba and blooded him fraternally.

There, cheerfully ensconced, he sat each day listening, looking and learning. Peter and Eddie greeted gaping students' gombeen glances with numbed expletives. Beating back doubts, they treated Joseph with boyish naturalness. As the first trembling week made way for the second, so too did school notes cram closed such certainty that at the Sunday dinner he voiced loud his news, 'D'ye realize that I'm looking forward to tomorrow.' Cemeteries contained the broken bones of his brothers crippled by cerebral palsy, they cackled and babbled their nude way through life, they verily died at birth and asked for nothing but fond love. Now he was resurrecting them and schooling their bones, asleep so very long, to come with him and bear witness that crones caused their banishment.

School life drained candid hearsay, but bread kneaded by Cassandra banked love's medley. Cambered, Joseph ceased to waste fears, school was cradling him and fading sadness zested cells of lenient mercy. Vested bedfellows nearly branded him fool, now civil friends were about to see him scale the Matterhorn. Carefully he noted students' burgeoning grasp of gesticulated communication, hackneyed imagination trod new terrain, lifting meaning from sighs, eyes and babbled cries.

School never baled him by greedily giving homework to Joseph. Wasting his crisis-rescued time doing homework would have meant strict garnering of tasted experiences could not be recorded by mind or muse. Feasting on created assertion Joseph grasped his beast-feasted-belly, and bibs-bedecked he bashfully brought forth droned, bespoked letters bested onto a page by a bent, nursed and crudely given nod of his stubborn head. As he typed he blundered like a young foal strayed from his mother. His own mother cradled his head but he mentally gadded here and there in fields of swishing grass and pursed wildness. His mind was darting under beech copper-mulled, along streams calling out his name, he hised and frollicked but his mother called it spasms. Delirious with the falling words plopping onto his path he made youth reel where youth was meant to stagnate. Such were Joseph's powers as he gimleted his words onto white sheets of life. Hands hanging loose by his side, electric pulses shooting through his body he just nodded and nodded typing numb-lost language onto his spores-bedecked altar. Sometimes his head shot back on his shoulders crashing like a mallet into his mother's face. She struggled with her feelings at times like that, greatly she understood, but he oftentimes sensed from her fingers that her battle was similar to his. Nutshelled fables he painted before her bent body and silent gaze, bashfully she read credit where he read acclaim.

Fashioned friendship he now felt beaming across his playground called Mount Temple. He felt the glow lighting glimmering candles in his boy's mind. But he was like a shark in blood-powered waters, he was forever hunting for friends, hunting for love. As pupils called to one another in friendship his name began to cross their corded denim world.

Rare was the youthful despair now, as glad Joseph went his way. Dead dreams seen in perspective carried a purpose, they immunized him against vested frockcoated feasibility of failure. Brash credence in himself nosedived before but now he certainly felt able to take on students and talk to them whatever way he could. Washed thoroughly in new-found hope he guaranteed himself, no wacky student-assessment is going to come between me and school life as every able-bodied boy knows it. Mesmerized by a lot of progress, clinging still to his boys and girls of weary youth, he now fostered fresh friends in Mount Temple.

Peers, civic minded, called to visit him at home. Casting dry frantic faith in their motivation, Joseph did his best to verify what craw-thumper voiced his name to them. Did they come to visit him out of sympathy or out of frantic compliance with the motivating influence of others? Thus he deliberated, thus did he find who his real friends were.

Naturally he sensed his family's frantic assessment of distress in his life, they heard his laughter now but read the cost, especially through his exhaustion on returning home from school. Many an evening Nora saw fit to heave Joseph from his wheelchair and place him in a big soft armchair in the kitchen where he stole a cosy sleep after his busy day in school.

Nested by a happy home Joseph continued to write. He recounted his experiences, his escried creeds and his crested benediction in typewritten words selected especially to describe a glorious bountiful nightmare. He saw life recoil before him, and using the third person he rescued poor sad boyhood and casting himself inside the frame of crippled Joseph Meehan he pranked himself as a storyteller, thereby casting renown on himself by dangling disability before the reader. Look, he begged, look deep down; feel, he begged, sense life's limitations; cry, he begged, cry the tears of cruel frustration; but above all he begged laughter, laugh, he pleaded, for lovely laughter vanquishes raw wounded pride.

Sally forward Joseph Meehan called an inner nested notion and gently heeding he damn-well forward sallied. Zoo-caged, he cracked the communication barrier by schooling hamfisted facial muscles to naturally smile on cue, and by combining smiles with nods of his head he found human warmth in the response of a candid smile from some girls and boys in Class 1L.

As Mount Temple absorbed him into its system, home became his corner for creating noise as he freely backed signs and mimes with sounds as great as mama, adaa, Eonn, to croaks, babbles or laughter expressed against intakes of breath. Crass comment always came to best his faith in his talkstyle. Churning out music as vocalized music gained many a cider-sweet comment from his family, 'Shut-up Joseph, we can't hear our ears with you roaring.' On one occasion Joseph found himself having to reprimand his own mother. She was baking bread while at the same time listening to Beethoven's Moonlight Sonata, and seeing how much his mother was enjoying it Joseph listened too. It harnessed his voice into expressing how calm and beautiful the music made him feel, but his vocalization spoiled the calmness of the moment for Nora. 'Ssh Joseph, don't be shouting,' she said. Music or no music, Joseph made his stand. He ordered her to sit down and looking her straight in the face he in his fashion told her firmly 'I wasn't shouting, I was singing.' A slow smile sneaked across her face and then she burst out laughing. The sound quivered slightly, but as she got up to walk away she said through a tear-choked voice 'I'm very sorry, I'll know better the next time.' But then, typical of her frankness, she came back and hurled cold water on the delicacy of the moment by adding: 'I'll continue to say shut up but you can respond as you see fit.' Joseph continued his singing, his talking and his 'see fit' answers, verily denying assessment of his communication as being anything other than perfectly normal for him.

Casts of boys and girls masked Joseph Meehan's brass-nosed beacon. Assisting him in school by wheeling him from classroom to classroom, they badgered him to deem acute cinctures of uselessness as creepy to able-bodied nasty students. 'Don't mind them Joseph,' they whispered, as stretching for a dry tissue stored in the pocket of his chair they wiped dry the saliva as it dribbled from the corners of his mouth. Tracking him always were his frantic new friends Peter Nicholson, Nora Byrne, Frank Ryan, Noel Canavan, Louise Higgins and Rosemary Taplin. Cain and Abel zealously cajoled all of the twenty-eight members of Class 1L to accept their sad brother, useless though he seemed.

As day followed day in school, so too did daring sceptics voice loud their childish opinions. Joseph was now getting used to hearing himself discussed. Quite openly students discussed his defects, and certain as they were of his non-ability to understand, they decided to be as vociferous as if he were not really present. They wondered if the cripple wore a nappy and longed to be able to examine him and find out for certain. Then they discussed his lack of intelligence. They chose tags by which they would rate him. They bandied about the words weirdo, eejit, cripple, dummy and mental defective. They decided he shouldn't be in a school for normal children and set about ridiculing the headmaster and staff for being the innocents they apparently were. Posing as a fool, Joseph listened and learnt how other students saw him. Sometimes he would react and suddenly hold up his head very high and gaze long and searchingly at them. All in vain, they grinned in ridicule at his seeming sensible.

Schooldays were sweetened by sugarstick fate. Unlike the sick chicken story, not everyone picked on the defenceless boy. Joseph Meehan knew what friendship really meant the day he saw Frank Ryan take action. Joseph and Frank were sitting having a break from class when a conversation going on a bit away suddenly begun to sink in. Needless to say, the cripple was under review, and deducing that Joseph couldn't stand it any longer, Frank grabbed hold of the handles of the wheelchair and made a beeline for the bunch of boy debaters. They scattered like frightened birds, but rounding on Frank's stupidity they failed to take his hint. Frank waited until he was outside and seating himself on the grass, he looked up into Joseph's face saying, 'How do ya stick it, Joseph? God I'd love to give them a kick in the puss, but then what good would that do? Ya can't beat sense into the bastards, they see themselves as normal and the assholes can't see further than their own noses. Lord I'd love to bleedin' bash them.' Joseph wasn't at all hurt, but Frank's defence had him twisted into knots of silent giggling. Outwardly though, he was attempting to flow understanding to Frank. He was trying to beg forgetfulness on Frank's part, for in his short life he had already discovered that forgetfulness fugues tongues and balms words. Shortly afterwards Frank confided his findings to Joseph's friends, but it was Peter Nicholson who clinched the issue by declaring, 'What the feck about them. Just wait Joseph, we'll open their bloody eyes yet.' Would that he could cheer, but instead Joseph fumbled with his feelings for friends such as his.

Life was a constant series of challenges to the disabled boy, but determined not to be beaten he faced each day as though greatly blessed by fate. School had but its place in his scheme, his writing nudged for attention too. Boy though he was, his need to find time to express his thoughts bullied and badgered constantly. Fashioned as a boy fool by thistle-topped grinning boys and girls, he was determined to outwit them at their own game.

As the school year progressed, so too did his autobiography. Gradually he chased filmy pomegranate secrets onto typewritten pages. He attempted to rescue crippled man from pits of oblivion and set about shattering the sacred-held image of handicap as being godsent. Assessing the old beliefs, he found them cruelly wanting. He voiced his doubts about God being bothered about spastics; rather he set about giving credit where credit was due. Restfully reassured by his new friends, Joseph now nominated God in a new light, 'Man is God hesitant and God is Man hesitantly trying to help.'

Joseph dredged his brain and battled his body. Slowly the clumsily typed words decorated his pages. Desperately he bullied, greatly he suffered. Chugging afflicted history furnaced by frescoed fear, he bygoned the past and cheered the future. Weary from his battle to win friends, yet wearier still from his battle to whet words from his entrapped mind, he felt moidered but uncrushed. He had his mind set on the closing date for the Spastics Society Literary Contest. His poetry had the previous year won for him a special prize and now he declared his intention to submit his autobiography for the current contest. Will it be in time he thought, will it be good enough he spoiled. Weaned by pummelled blows to his conscious babbling cries, he now wrote the gilded story of his survival in an alien, silent, lock-jawed world.

Came the day, and Joseph had at last typed the final words of his life story, but now he faced another problem. A postal strike froze the hopes of the twelve-year-old boy. Yet again though, he found able-bodied man ready to help him. His neighbour took his letter to his place of employment at Dublin Airport and begged an Aer Lingus pilot to post the brown envelope in London. Not able to thank either of the men, he bowed and murmured a mincing 'bless them'.

Boyhood became blissful now, friends became pals and school became relaxed. The debt due to John Medlycott the headmaster became enormous for now his dearest wish was coming true, his wheelchair-bound pupil was but another pupil, no more than that, no less. Craving freedom to be himself but polestarred nonetheless, Joseph was happier than he ever could convey. Communication was now two-way, his pals talked to him, he communicated with them. They had discovered the secret by which to chat with their silent friend, so it was nothing strange for them to try lifting his head by sticking a finger under his chin and begging, 'Lift up your feckin' head until we see what you're saying.' Exactly thus did they get a feedback from him and thus it became completely normal for them to relate to his eyes pooling as they were his lifeline with their world. As conversation tactics developed they learnt that youthful adventures interested him just as much as able-bodied them. So too did misdemeanours beckon him since he realized that he could now bank on pals to help him make his getaway. Casking Joseph's cries of excitement and chortles of laughter by placing their hand severely over his mouth, they helped him to suppress his nervous reaction. By silencing him thus, they enabled him to join them as they hid from teachers, fellow students or even the headmaster. Mottled allotments breaded wonderful love in Joseph Meehan's new world. The boys and girls belonging to his circle proved imaginative, jest-filled, devoted (but not mawkish), verved and sincere. They now felt sure of themselves and harassed nosey juniors to 'scram off to hell ya gawkin' fecker'.

Boys will be boys, and disabled though he was, he did what every schoolboy does – he sat each day sizing up his teachers. He watched their style, their teaching skill, their dedication and the front they put on, trying as they were to give the impression that they were the great and absolute authority on their subject. He watched them discipline their class of twelve or thirteen-year-old boys and girls. His was a co-educational, interdenominational school, so as he watched he noted teachers walking the tightrope between sexual understanding and giddy students' hang-ups. He watched boys trying to lord it over girls and he watched girls boldly challenging boys to grow up, be your age, and then as if to beat home their challenge they destroyed the imagined superiority of the boys by coming away ahead of them in classwork and exams. The teachers rarely took sides in the boys-versus-girls debates, rather they bemusedly watched the first hint of understanding developing among the first years.

The modern buildings of Mount Temple were all single-storeyed and flat-roofed. Great long corridors blossomed between the various school sections. The first corridor was tinted golden-yellow, the middle corridor purple-hued and the third yelled grass-green. Frenzied activity made Cromwell-destruction look nub-notioned, for frenzy has comic-book colours that history books lack. Mornings in Mount Temple corridors, though fearsome in thoughtful bedlam, no longer nested fear for Joseph and his wheelchair. He now felt at home and in fact was comforted by being able to share the mêlée with all of those normal students. But winter days in great, glad school froze him to the marrow of his bone. His healthy body could not fight the cursed cold. His feet assumed a dead weight as cold spread along his limbs. By lunchtime his was a marble-cold body. But great mercy had a way of hearing his blood slow down. His mother detected that his body seemed cold beyond the usual when she brought him to the toilet one frosty March day. 'Are you always this cold?' she asked, and he showed her his feet explaining in his fashion that the feet get cold first and then the chill sets in. Next day Joseph was comfortable dressed as he now was in thermal underwear and an extra pair of socks. That more than matched his lack of mobility. Freed from cold, Joseph now faced the draughts in the corridors with a devil-may-care attitude.

Spring cast a bright mantle over the lean landscape, hiccuping green life into Mount Temple's foliage. It gladdened the heart of staff and students alike, but in Joseph's heart it no longer spelt hopelessness. Now it sang cuckoo-songs of mystical-hulled music. In celebrating spring the school held their annual Open Day. Great colour joined forces with nature as art students exhibited their paintings all around their art room, all along the mall, even overflowing into the long-walled corridors. Great collages of handcrafts stood on exhibition: chairs, tables, assorted pottery, metalwork and for the academically-minded, long trestle tables showed their well researched and laid-out projects. Regretting that he was unable to yield anything, Joseph set about admiring the skills of others. Crestfallen he resolved that he would one day have something to show for his class and his years.

Mead flowed through schooldays as the year latticed seeping thoughtful Fridays. June wound roses in and out of Joseph's hope-filled notions. He had borne his wombed life, he had hoped in doubt but was proved wrong, he asked for kindness and was given love in bucketfuls. Now at schoolfriends' hands he glanced in awe.

School ended in sunny happy June. Mr Medlycott broke the silence in class by coming on the intercom. 'Attention please', he begged and then continuing with his announcements he called out the dates for the Intermediate and Leaving Certificate exam-inations. He announced the dates for the house exams and then he announced the closing date for the school holidays. With his announcement came excitement. Giddiness set in. Joseph sneered comradely as boys and girls jeered. He sneered with them as they made their cheeky comments about the 'ould school' the 'ould headmaster', 'He can sod off', 'Go stuff himself now'. They belittled everyone and everything, but it was only bantering, they were excited by the thought of holidays and by the pleasure-filled freedom, which beckoned ahead.

Three long months of holidays stretched ahead. Free to remi-nisce, he glanced back over his first year in an able-bodied folk's school. No more clockwatching he rejoiced, no more hurried breakfasts, no more fleeting glances at the toilet wishing he had time to see if he wanted to go, no more days in school when he wished he could go but had to wait till lunchtime or evening at home, no more pangs of hunger as he watched boys biting into big juicy apples or rummaging in crisp bags or slugging bottles of orange juice, no more having to look for understanding when his fist flattened a poor bugger's nose, no more apologetic looks when his fingers grasped fistfuls of girlish curls, or even worse when his hand gripped a girl's skirt or beat against her bosom earning for him he was sure Yvonne's comment always, 'Let go, you sex mechanic!'

CHAPTER FOUR

THE STIRRING OF THE MUSE

JOSEPH gulped down his new-found freedom, schooldays had ended but somehow he felt sad. He missed his friends but now looked towards his sister's arrival. Yvonne was away at a convent boarding school situated on the banks of the River Shannon. She frequented his dreams often but now she was due home for her holidays. He was used to peace and calm, but when Yvonne came home he saw bedlam take over. Music blared now where heretofore it played at a normal volume. The phone rang constantly and long gigglesome conversations took place on it. Pop music was ever the menu now, news bulletins were kept brief, but parents were now fighting for their rights to hear the long indigestible meanderings so hated by the young. Joseph watched and egged on his sister, not that Yvonne needed much encouraging, but now that he had a voice he lived for the hell of it, he frenetically freed himself and hollered for more.

Coping with two rebellious teenagers were two placid realists. Matthew and Nora sensed how case-hardened young folk become. They watched as their bold daughter challenged her spastic brother to be as normal in his outlook as she was normal in her treatment of him. Yvonne never babied Joseph, she fought fairly and squarely with him. Classed now as a boy-writer, she had forecast what he could do many years before he ever managed to write a sibling creation. Her peopled poem entitled 'My Brother' called numb chiding to languageless Joseph's locked indelible word pleonasm. School studies nobbled her creative thinking, so it was under her pillow that Nora found the beautiful, breastfilled poem. Yvonne had been home for her weekend break from strict boarding school routine and had returned to Banagher by the Shannon leaving a cast of woolsoft beauty beneath her deep-lolled, down-filled pillow.

Yvonne was happy for her brother when eventually he broke free from his locked lonely silence. She never had any great difficulty understanding his nodding-headed, eye-darting language. Measuring herself against him always, she composed beautiful poems and he wrote boyish poems. When recognition moved her brother towards the title poet she hugged him in warm reassurance. Now she watched and waited with him to see how his autobiography fared in London.

Together the Meehans waited. Matthew, a psychiatric nurse by profession but a farmer at heart, worked in the community. For many years he had worked in St Loman's Hospital, Mullingar while at the same time living on and farming his Corcloon acres. He honestly strove to make life better for his patients in the hospital, spending long, long hours attending to their troubled foibled lives. Matthew worked a day-on, day-off rota so it served to allow him time to run his farm. Deeming themselves genuine rednecks they farmed their fertile fields. Cabby drivers bombed by circumstances, they lugged millstoned Joseph up and down through the fenced land. Weary but never defeated by fate, they brought their disabled child with them everywhere they went. When he was too small yet for a wheelchair, they placed Joseph's little pummeled chair into the bright blue wheelbarrow, and with Yvonne and Bruce the collie, they took turns wheeling their only boy all around the farm. The chariot often bumped against a hillock, heeling over and tossing the rider out on top of his head. With looks of sureness they promised to be more careful as assuaging his hurt pride they loaded anew their passenger and set off to investigate and explain nature to their children. Agreeing between themselves, they lifted their child from his chair and allowed him access to birds' nests, anthills and sheep farts, letting him kick asunder the gas-dust filling of the puffball fungi. As the river ran through the farm, Joseph was allowed to paddle in it, freezing himself to death in the cold spring water. He was helped to fish for pinkeens and to stay stockstill while searching for a trout in a direction wildly fingered by whispering Yvonne. Such was the scene in Joseph's certain childhood, such was the year played from crab-apple blossoms to fresh-chocolate brown turf-cutting, from haycock fun to foolish dog's rabbit run. The berried fraughans* coated the banks of Dublin's mountain boreens,† but as yet Joseph was ignorant of their existence. He all childishly thought that Westmeath held solemn pleasure, only Westmeath, the county of his ancestors.

But crestfallen by crippled freedom he pulled as best he could. Sensing his heinous horribleness of hope he cried once, once only.

Nora never gobbled up her son. Sensing how very difficult life was going to be, she spoke resurrecting hope when there was no hope at all. Feeling his frustration she looked on in silence. Fashioned babyhood was bubbling his broken heart's hollowness. He was only three years old but he cried the tears of a sad man. Creeked now, his tears coursed down his face but better now, reasoned his mother, than fobbed off for future festering.

Sun shone that day long ago in Corcloon. Yvonne was gone to school. Asleep in his blue bed Joseph looked the picture of pleasant childlike thimblework. Nora serenely simpered as she lifted him. Washed and powdered he sat on her lap. Fondly she slipped the geansai‡ over his blonde head. His head tilted boldly forward then suddenly it shot backwards. He faced his mother. He gazed his hurt gaze, lip protruding, eyes busy in conversation. He ordered her to look out the window at the sunshine. He looked hard at her ear ordering her to listen to the birds singing. Then jumping on her knees he again asked her to cock her ear and listen to the village children out at play in the school yard. Now he jeered himself. He showed her his arms, his legs, his useless body. Beckoning his tears he shook his head. Looking at his mother he blamed her, he damned her, he mouthed his cantankerous why, why, why me? Distracted by his youthful harshness of realization

*similar to blackcurrants.
†country lanes.
‡jersey.

she tried to distract him. Lifting him in her arms she brought him outside into the farmyard. 'Come on till I show you the calves,' she coaxed. His lonely tears rushed even faster. He knew why she tried to divert his boyish questioning. He childishly determined not to look at the calves and shaking his head he gazed the other way. His mother tried again. 'Look over at the lambs,' she said, pointing at the sheep feeding at their trough in the field. He cried so loud he brought her to her senses. 'Alright,' she said, 'we'll go back inside and talk.' Placing him in his chair she then sat down and faced her erstwhile boy, yes, her golden-haired accuser. Meanwhile he cried continuously, conning himself that he had beaten her to silence. Looking through his tears he saw her as she bent low in order to look into his eyes. 'I never prayed for you to be born crippled,' she said. 'I wanted you to be full of life, able to run and jump and talk just like Yvonne. But you are you, you are Joseph not Yvonne. Listen here Joseph, you can see, you can hear, you can think, you can understand everything you hear, you like your food, you like nice clothes, you are loved by me and Dad. We love you just as you are.' Pussing still, snivelling still, he was listening to his mother's voice. She spoke sort of matter-of-factly but he blubbered moaning sounds. His mother said her say and that was that. She got on with her work while he got on with his crying.

The decision arrived at that day was burnt forever in his mind. He was only three years in age but he was now fanning the only spark he saw, his being alive and more immediate, his being wanted just as he was.

Dread-filled fretting marked Joseph Meehan's scene that day, but that scene and that day looked out through his eyes for the rest of his life. Comfort came in child-like notions, his clumsy body was his, but molested by mother-love he looked lollying looks at his limbs and liked Joseph Meehan.

Because he liked himself his youth sidled along with the minimum of grumbling. His real inspiration came from his father. He watched him struggle against seeming distress. Testing his son's strength he found him wanting. The boy heard his father referring to him as 'not having the makings of a farmer'. But his father had the makings of a seanchai* and he never knew it. Placing his wobbling son on his knee he recited poetry, told nursery rhymes and later on bawdy vulgar stories. Joseph's mind was wallowing in his father's mire of memories. His asides always began with the question, 'Did you ever hear the story ...?' His stories were short, seamed with fun but thought-provoking for a boy child.

Sameness of scene was mesmerized by his father's cheery fencing. 'Did you ever hear about the little donkey?' he asked one day, as together the father and son sat by the fire. Joseph looked enquiringly at his dad. Then turning the boy around to face him he recited the first poem that Joseph ever heard. 'It's about a little new-born foal donkey,' he added. And so the boy listened as his father created the image of a donkey:

> 'One day old,
> His head was too big
>   For his neck to hold.
>
> 'His legs were shaky,
>   And long and loose;
> They rocked and staggered,
>   And weren't much use.'

Joseph listened to the whole poem, he formed the image of the little wobbly donkey in his mind. He looked at his own limbs, his head lolled back, the stirring of the muse took root that day.

Nobody butted in when Matthew recited his vivid stories. They were never warned in advance that his mind charted lovely creative-lying language. His eye would spot fresh reminders of hidden stored poetry, and true to notional nurturing he'd borrow lines which would unconsciously nurse his family into his luxurious landscape. So it was that his children culled musical notation, intricate thought patterns and a merry love of writing. Literature was never mentioned. Creative thought was stirring, but the natural surroundings were country landscapes and life revolved

*storyteller.

around farm animals and farming chores. Nobody was aware of what was happening and writers and poets were seldom mentioned. Love of history though threshed out names of Irish poets like Francis Ledwidge, Padraic Colum, Joseph Mary Plunkett, William Alingham, Yeats or Patrick Kavanagh. Matthew had fine recall and a mention of the Great War served but to give him a chance to talk about Francis Ledwidge.

Looking on and listening, silent Joseph boyishly prayed, asking Father God for help. Will you help me to use this hand he begged, as childishly he indicated his left hand. He wanted to be able to say what was going on in his mind. Fears for his nested offerings bred caesuras of despair. But mundane life, yes mundane life never heard his cry. Father God viewed his left hand and deduced that freedom to communicate nutshelled secrets heralded long lonely fumbling ahead. Mocked by disappointment, the boy healed his hand by rubbing it against his play things or giving it to the dog to lick.

Creaming bonny joy from servile Hecuba, young Joseph dreamt and dreamt. Youth schooled his resolve to breathe his poetry in written form. Dead dreams were shed from his brain, while new ideas cogged dreams of the future.

Frills made from spooned secrets hurrahed in his mind. Lifting his head from his night pillow he mesmerized himself by plumbing the pleasures of life. He thought of lovely lines of poetry that he had picked up from his dad's wanderings. He followed the marching armies of the Confederates and the Yankies and boyishly cheered bravery when:

> Up rose old Barbara Fritchie then,
> Bowed with her fourscore years and ten;
> Bravest of all in Frederick town,
> She took up the flag the men hauled down.
> 'Shoot, if you must, this grey old head,
> But spare your country's flag,' she said.

Fleetfooting from Frederick town he crested his mind to Rome to listen as:

The hinges whined to the shutters shaking
When clip–clop–clep came a horse-hoof raking
The stones of the road at Caesar's gate.

Thinking of snow the young boy could nestle into his pillow and casually call up his dad's timorous thesis:

> Nothing is quite so quiet and clean
> As snow that falls in the night,
> And isn't it jolly to jump from bed
> And find the whole world white.

A poem for every remembrance, vivid–themed and cast away, insured an oral resurrecting under a wobbling voice.

Matthew Meehan meddled in medleys of cheery but breath-takingly beautiful thought. Words seemed his tools of trade as he ferreted for mollification in his bondaged world. Matthew would be the very last to sense that his broad rambling murmurings might be beneficial to his children. He was reared under his father's tutelage but he never detected that his own erudite mind nutshelled evergreen bunting.

Joseph Meehan had not yet broken his silence, but unknown to his parents he ebbed and neaped under his father's flow. Not yet able to write his creative thoughts, he waxed and waned in secret. His father rarely hollered at his son; he thought to himself that friendship brought his son nearer to normality. Joseph appreciated their friendship, never happier than when his dad got vulgar. Carrying his son down the stairs in the morning Matthew could be heard asking:

> 'Here hath been dawning another blue day
> Think, wilt thou let it slip useless away?'

But on arrival at the downstairs toilet his thoughts would turn vulgar as placing his son on the seat he'd relax him by saying:

> I'll tell you a story,
> A story that's true,
> An old man died
> And his belly was blue:

I'll tell you another,
A story you can trust,
If it wasn't for your bum
Your belly'd burst.

then he'd join with his son in merry laughter.

CHAPTER FIVE

THE EIGHT-LEGGED PONY

CHRISTMAS-TIMED, the young boy's gossamer gift snuggled still in his cubbyholed mine. He slyly hugged himself and his secret. Tingling sounds hesitated but malice held rein-tight grip on his boy's bondring.

Years budded hushed, bubbling bubbly bubbles, but bubbles burst and leave no trace. The father tried to nylon-thread his love for his broken breastplate boy by rescuing history in plonk of poetic but nomdeplumed, headgritted charting.

Nutshelling life, Yvonne headed her brother towards his dreadful goal. She cradled his head when he was sick but when he was well she gave him hell. She got a lovely speckled Connemara foal as a birthday gift from her dad and mam. The spiteful bitch lorded it over her crippled brother. 'Now here,' she crowed, 'is something I don't have to share with you.' She was seven years old and he was five. Both children watched the foal become pony and both children watched the wild pony being broken into a beautiful, sleeky jumper. Breasted as normal Yvonne learnt to ride. There she sat in her burnished, shiny saddle upon the back of her very own Sally. Joseph sat in his little purple chair with the red leather pummel nestling between his legs. Seated thus he certainly could not slither from his seat. Resting thus he frowned at his sister, now centre-stage and stealing the limelight from him. Week followed week and Yvonne became gracefully confident as she rode well and jumped better. Brothers cannot watch on forever, so Joseph nodded towards himself. Yvonne refused and rode by. He called her again and again but she rode by. He felt like giving up but determined to look hurt and bruised. She hurried by. He hung his head the next time, hung it low and didn't ask. She rode towards him, stopped and yielded. 'Look here brat, I'll give you one ride, that's all,' she said. 'No use yelling when you have to get down. It's my pony, my pony, do you hear?' His real battle was over, he felt he could ride if only he could get into the saddle. Nora heard the row between her children, heard Yvonne laying down the law under her brother's nose. She went out to the haggard calling Matthew to come join her. Between them the parents grumbled at their son wanting to get up so high. Between them though they deposited their crippled boy in the sinewless, slippy saddle. One on either leg they held him, a hand each gripping his arms. Together they balanced him. He nodded, he was ready. Matthew asked the pony for him and off he went.

Stirrups hung loose but headstrong boy that he was, he hurt from fear of failure. His pattern of life buttoned hard fear of failure. Now here he was on the Connemara pony, her gun-metal-grey mane falling gracefully near his nose, her sable coat gleaming with health, her ears standing like steeples before his eyes and her breath blowing bygones from his mind. Pulling on the reins on either side, the hidden strengths of his parents guided the pony around the hollow ground. Sally walked slowly, the parents walked just as slowly. Joseph got uneasy. He demanded to speed her up. Bespoked sounds hollered, he heralded his kudos before crowing parents ever got a chance to speak. Frightened for their child's safety, Matthew and Nora ran at either side of dappled Sally for now boy-jockey Joseph was egging them on to trot faster. Chortling with brave ignorance he was nudging them to go for the jump. They picked up cunning Joseph's signals and not having time to argue they trotted towards the jump.

Up and over went the eight-legged pony, bearded jockey hunched on Sally's neck. Beast and boy were emanating a great wondrous Ness-like vraiment. Thirsty notoriety homme-like hic-cuped individual hollyberries on all robbed moments of holly-leafed life.

Lessons looked everyone in the face that day. Parents yielded to their kinky son and learned how not to restrain his boy's spirit of adventure and broad brave unction. Yvonne yielded to her human heart's murmuring and discovered yet again that her brother was never defeated, never a weakling. Sackful of happiness Joseph too learned a lesson, he hefty in needs no longer begrudged his sister Sally. He decorated himself as a jockey, but it was her tender heart that provided his steed that beautiful day.

The mere mention of a boat gave Nora nervous worry and fear. But when Matthew announced that he was going to make his own boat she laughed, knowing full well that she had nothing to worry about. So the boat helmed by her husband was an experience she would never have. She had so often heard Matthew say 'Ah sure there's nothing to it, I could make that myself'. And she would reply, 'Oh yea, will you make it before or after you finish the aeroplane?' Matthew's mind was full of inventive notions, but carrying out his plans was something else indeed.

Nora thought no more about the boat. She had gone to Mullingar to do shopping and have her hair done. But true to his form, Matthew took action when he got the coast clear. Nora, on her return, was driving in along the driveway when in her line of vision a tall tree suddenly disappeared from view. She knew she was sober, she knew what she saw, but when she saw her husband's sheepish, sweaty smile she knew the worst. True to her form Nora played it cool; after all she reasoned, there's a long way between a freshly felled tree and a watertight boat.

Matthew sawed his tree into lengths and Nora had to hide her misgivings as she helped to roll the lengths up onto the trailer. With the sawmill in mind, Matthew set off for Mullingar to have his larch tree cut into laths. Allowing time for the timber to season, Matthew then painted each lath with creosote. Now he was ready for his royal job. Assessing his needs he lined up his tools. Then like a mare about to foal he chose his site.

The month when the boat-building got underway was May. The weather was handpicked for the solemn undertaking. It was the finest summer in fifty years. Bold Matthew cradled his scheme of building in his mind, while with each day that passed the shape and bulge of the boat grew to lovely proportions. Matthew was in his element. He chatted with his lone audience, he explained what he was doing, why he was doing it and showed the young boy the end result of each tool's job. Then quietness would reign although punctured sometimes by his hammering. Always happy, the father sang. He sang every ould song, every ould come-all-ye that ever nestled in his brain. Then tired of singing he'd talk of the awful heat of the sun. As usual he'd throw an aside:

> Christy Maguire pissed in the fire,
> The fire was too hot so he pissed in the pot.

Then throwing caution to the wind he'd breathe hard, hammer in another nail and glancing a wicked glance at his son he'd venture:

> The lord and the lady lived in a spout,
> The lord let off a banger and blew the lady out.

Immediately then he'd reverse his role and his poetry would turn to the sublime with his reciting 'The Rime Of The Ancient Mariner' or Sir Walter Scott's:

> The stag at eve had drunk his fill,
> Where danced the moon on Monan's rill.

Nora catered for the thirst of the boat-builder and his helpmate. She ran a shuttle service supplying cold welcome drinks along with big nourishing sandwiches. She couldn't but admire the creative handiwork as it progressed before her sceptical eyes. Matthew sat down to eat, all the while though eyeing his masterpiece. Then with a rub of his hand to his mouth he returned to his task.

Banana-shaped but beautiful, the boat now needed oars. The whole operation complete, the artist painted his model. He chose grey for the colour because, nervously afraid of failure, he reckoned in vain that a grey boat would be less conspicuous at the bottom of the river.

The day dawned when a great event was about to take place. A boat of a man's dreams was about to be launched. But he needed a baler for fear of a leak and a baler he found in young Pat Earley. Now all was in readiness for breathless launching.

The boat was loaded on the trailer and off they set. The whole

Meehan family and their neighbour. Their destination, a lovely broad tributary of the Boyne. Treating the boat with kid-glove attention, they lowered it down into the Yellow River. Matthew hurriedly got into it but on seeing the water seep in he called Pat to the rescue. Pat hurriedly baled and all was grand. 'Are ye getting in?' asked the wily sailor. Joseph nodded and bowed. Nearing the bank Matthew stretched up and lifted the chair-clad boy down into the boat.

Nora and Yvonne stood anxiously watching the maiden voyage of Matthew's dream. Pat baled at his best while Matthew rowed at his smoothest. Joseph's chair fitted nicely between the seats and with nothing up but his blonde head the boat sailed him along. The proud crew showed off rowing their lovely fourteen-foot boat up and back under cowardly view.

Wyvern-wise now, Nora hid her failure to trust her husband's handicraft by claiming that she needed to be on the bank to rescue the sailors if they got into difficulties. As well as that she claimed someone ought to be left to collect the insurance money. But Matthew made allowances for her – after all he was wise to her fear of a watery grave.

Life on a farm asks for constant vigilance. Matthew Meehan worked hard to lighten the chores for his helpmate. But life goes on whether man is there or not. Joseph watched the teamwork of his parents. When her husband was on duty in his hospital, Nora did double duty at home. She home-kept but she farm-kept too. The walls of the kitchen asked for inspection as Joseph spent time waiting for his mother to finish milking the cows, feeding the calves, foddering the cattle and sheep and feeding the poultry. Every so often she dropped in to have a word with Joseph, to tell him what stage she was at, to tell him that, 'The ould bitch of a cow nearly spilt the bucket of milk', or that she'd have to 'keep an eye out for a ewe that showed signs of yeaning'. He nodded in understanding, knowing full well that she was anxious to finish and return to her housework.

Rescued moments all wobbled great boyish inventions of thought. Sitting in the kitchen, Joseph played wonderful games using the pictures that Nora had drawn for her children.

Hessian-tied he rode the broomstick behind the black-caped witch. Her aspect of defiance as she brayed her querulous cry heralded boyish defiance in his heart. Her broom cradled her black cat while her vindictive laugh cancelled out the luck he associated with a black cat. Mouthing his instructions he gagged the witch and begged the cat to grant luck to him in his search for fame.

The next picture was a grey elephant. It was a big drawing and really put the elephants in the zoo in the penny-ha'penny place. It described every feature of the great lumbering beast but Nora's drawing hinted not of the animal's intelligent memorizing of hurts.

The farmhouse kitchen unites farm and husbandry of family and farm animals. Everything emanates from the kindly kitchen. Joseph freed fealty of failure as he glanced umbilical glances at the word pictures arranged around the walls of the desert-dry kitchen. The paintings were stuck to the walls. Over the fireplace lingered the pointy-hatted witch riding her broom against the moon, like a scudding cloud she flew, nobility knew not her. The grey elephant looked down on him from the end wall, it demanded glances nestling as it was on the same wall as the picture of the Sacred Heart. Wonder joined him as ducking the all-knowing and searching eye of God he turned his gaze away, by the way glancing at his grey whitehead calf and his dad's tractor. Would that he could hide, but overtly feigning interest in the other pictures he glanced admiringly at his chalk-coloured calf. He ignored God's picture and instead remembered the day he chose the grey whitehead calf as his. It was mart day in Maynooth and Matthew and Nora brought him to the sales. They bought five calves, but he got his spake in before his sister and bowed and bowed towards the grey whitehead heifer calf. Yvonne came home from school that evening and realizing that he had upstaged her, his sister said, 'The ould calf looks delicate, her coat is neither grey, blue nor red.' Still wishing to avoid the eyes of enquiring God, he sized up the picture of Matthew's red tractor. He sat behind the steering wheel and again mouthed his joy as with his dad holding his hands on the wheel he chugged his woeful way up and down and all around the big field. He thought he could smell the diesel in his nostrils, thought he could feel the bumpety bump of the tractor in motion, fringe blowing back he glanced anew through the black vapour belching from the funnel. Now where will I look wondered the musing boy, but he desperately wished to avoid looking into those lovely eyes. He had only one wall left but on glancing over at that he banged right up against the rush-plaited cross.

Several times he looked back at the end wall and now he gave in to those eyes. Snared, he too questioned young questioning. What am I going to do when I leave here, he voiced out loud. He reckoned that God would understand his mouthed words. He asked, never waiting for a hint of comfort. What will happen when I go to Dublin's Central Remedial Clinic School? What will become of me when I have nobody to understand my talkstyle? What will my teachers make of me? I'm afraid, are you listening, don't see and say nothing. I'm afraid, afraid of my life 'cause I won't have mam or dad or even Yvonne. I'll be on my own, my head falling back and forward, not able to talk, not able to hug myself when I get afraid. God, would you be afraid if you were me?

CHAPTER SIX

KNIFE USED

WINTER was wonderful in Corcloon. Farming was fun for children but hell for farmers. This was the very last winter on the farm. The Meehans were moving to the Big Smoke. The rednecks were going to meet the Molly Malones. It was all Joseph's fault. If he had come into the world head-first, weather could still be wonderful for kids in Corcloon. But he asked for trouble when he decided to lie crossways in his mother's womb, not just crossways but all relaxed on the broad of his back. He wasn't going anywhere, but life demanded to see him. Stalling, he had to be lifted from his cosy hammock, knife used to prize him out. Privately, he had decided to choose death, but fate decided otherwise.

About death there is no secret. Joseph Meehan knows that, after all he has been there and back. He dwelt among the gods for two fobbed hours but life clawed him back, copperfastened him and called him free.

Christened for his cross-bearing, he chalk-white weathered the avenues of babyhood. But nobody wounded like him could deserve a chance at life. Better dead said the crones, better dead said history, better jump in at the deep end decided her strong soul as she heard his crestfallen cry. His mother it was who treated him as normal, tumbled to his intelligence, tumbled to his eye-signalled talk, tumbled to the hollyberries, green yet, but holding promise of burning in red given time, given home.

Quietly Nora sought an expert opinion about her baby. She brought him to Dublin's Fitzwilliam Street. Quietly she entered

No. 9 and carrying Joseph in her arms came face to face with Dr Ciaran Barry. He listened quietly to a mother's story of how everything went wrong at her son's birth. It took two operations to save her, the first was to deliver her of her baby and the second was carried out to save herself. Such was the cost worked out that brought her to Dr Barry.

Watching and listening, the blue-eyed doctor heard of a mother's quiet observations of her son. He watched the inquisitive baby looking at him, looking all around his surgery, looking as though he could understand what his mother was saying. The baby was just seventeen months old.

Assessing him, the doctor wisely played games with the child. He blew into his eyes once but when Joseph heard him taking a deep breath he was ready for him and cutely closed his eyes. Then when the doctor failed to blow the boy opened his eyes to see what was wrong. The games cutely constructed never found Joseph wanting. Sure of his findings, the doctor agreed with Nora that her son seemed to have normal intelligence. Then the brave doctor advised the mother about the child's treatment. He told her about the Central Remedial Clinic. He suggested that the boy should have attention there for physiotherapy, speech therapy, occupational therapy and in time, schooling.

Now the time was come and Boyblue had to have his education. Fretting for himself, he didn't count the price paid by his family. Now they had to change their whole lifestyle, their whole outlook. Gone would be the great days exploring washed stones in the river or seeing ewes beating tomtom-fashion on the ground with their front legs as they sought to guard their lambs. Gone too the fun gyrating on the swing when the ropes became twisted or singing in concert with the Earley children as they staged outdoor shows on the hay bogey in the haggard. Never again would he witness huge hungry machines bite deep into the bog and then swing wide a great iron arm to drop a long long sausage of shiny wet turf on the ceannbhán-coated* bank. Never again the experiences of his childhood for now Dublin City was calling him, calling him to school.

*ceannbhán-bog cotton

Dull in Corcloon, the weather became milky-blue over Dublin. Their farm lay behind them. Yes, work purpled these dreadful decisive days. But Matthew and Nora Meehan never fostered feeble fear, never looked back, no longer asked life to loosen its hellish hold on their throats for now hurried preparations made grim future join forces with great promise in the hill-long road ahead.

Oil-filled burner replaced turf-burning stove when the Meehans moved up to Dublin. Gone was Sally, gone was the poultry, gone the bold lovely Earleys. Now new neighbours moved in and out of Clontarf, nobody missed them, nobody really knew them.

Time was of the essence in the big busy city. Dublin yelled breezy certainty, told tempting place names and remedied loneliness for Corcloon. But the Meehans were up to it, they settled in, started school, mimed old joys and minimized new problems.

Joseph was familiar with Clontarf. He had been visiting the clinic on Vernon Avenue ever since his infancy. Three times each week he had travelled the milkyway to the CRC for his sessions of physiotherapy and speech therapy. The family bought their new house near the clinic so that Joseph would be near his school.

Fears of not being understood were quashed before he ever started school when he met the psychologist, Criona Garvey. He gave her a demonstration of his bowing-headed, eye-pointing, foot-peddling language. She smiled and understood his signals. Then she started to test his intelligence.

Holding his breath he watched her lay out her brain posers, but on the instant he found the answers. He was enjoying himself and feeling very much at ease. She eventually cried halt, but he would have liked to go on until he couldn't go any further. Criona Garvey sat back in her chair and smiled. He looked enquiringly at the psychologist. She talked to him about starting school but with a smile she said, 'Joseph, if you don't make great progress then you will have to answer to me.'

Like the school, the founder was Hector-hearted. Joseph had seen her on one of his visits to the clinic, but when the classroom door flew open one day he failed to recognize the lady who blustered in. She was dressed in a paisley design, mustard-coloured dress and flat shoes. 'Good afternoon Lady Goulding,' chorused the pupils. 'Good afternoon children,' smiled the visitor. She stood talking with the teacher while Joseph sat looking at none other than Lady Valerie Goulding.

Hesitating at the door she smiled at the class and in a fluster she was gone. Her face remained before his mind's eye, her trestled truth shone from her gaze, her smile came from a soul-burst and he remembered that she had had a ladder in her stocking.

Crying with fear the first few days in school, now here sat the same boy laughing with Alan or Alex. Here he sat demanding to be understood and being eventually interpreted and then understood. Great joy jumped in Joseph's heart as he mastered his subjects, but he was still seeking an outlet for his cubby-holed writings.

Joseph was well used to all the weeping-Jesus comments about his cross. He was now trying to break free from society's charitable mould. He saw how others saw him but he wanted to show everyone how truly wrong they were. Fenced in on all sides he heard things he was never meant to hear and he saw things he was never meant to see. Now could he ever get his chance to let folk see what they never thought existed?

How do I conquer my body, mused the paralysed boy. Paralysed I am labelled, but can a paralytic move? My body rarely stops moving. My arms wage constant battle trying to make me look a fool. My smile which can be most natural, can at times freeze, thereby making me seem sad and uninterested. Two great legs I may have, but put my bodyweight on them and they collapse under me like a house of cards. How then can I convey to folk that the strength in my legs can be as normal as that of the strongest man? Such were boy Joseph's taunting posers, but he had one more fence that freezed his words while they were yet unspoken.

But fate was listening and fate it was that had frozen his freedom. Now could fate be wavering in her purpose? Credence was being given to his bowed perceptions – could fate avow him a means of escape?

Writing by hand failed. Typing festered hope. The typewriter was not a plaything. Boy Joseph needed to master it for the good of his sanity, for the good of his soul. Years had taught him the ins and outs of typewriting, but fate denied him the power to nod and hit the keys with his head-mounted pointer. Destruction secretly destroyed his every attempt to nod his pointer onto the keys. Instead great spasms gripped him rigid and sent his simple nod into a farcical effort which ran to each and every one of his limbs.

Eva Fitzpatrick had done years of duty trying to help Joseph to best his body. She told him everything she knew about brain damage and its effects. The boy understood, but all he could do was to look hard into her humble eyes and flick his own heavenwards in affirmation.

'Yes, you may have Joseph,' agreed his class teacher each week when Eva came to collect her pupil for his typing lesson. Away down the corridors they sauntered, the young teacher and her disabled student. Eva chatted while Joseph listened. Trying sometimes to have his say, he would mouth his words while looking back into her eyes.

Eva's room was crested by creative drawings. Her manner was friendly, outgoing, but inwardly she felt for her student as he struggled to typewrite. Her method of working necessitated that her pupil be relaxed so she chatted light-hearted banter as she all the while measured his relaxation. The chatting would continue, but when Joseph saw his teacher wheel the long mirror towards the typing table he knew that they were going to play typing gymnastics.

Together they would struggle, the boy blowing like a whale from the huge effort of trying to discipline his bedamned body. Every tip of his pointer to the keys of the typewriter sent his body sprawling backwards. Eva held his chin in her hands and waited for him to relax and tip another key. The boy and girl worked mightily, typing sentences which Eva herself gave as a headline to Joseph. Young Boyblue honestly gave himself over to his typing teacher. Gumption was hers as she struggled to find a very voluntary tip coming to the typewriter keys from his yessing head.

But for Eva Fitzpatrick he would never have broken free. His own mother had given up on him and decided that the typewriter was no help at all. She had put the cover on the machine and stored it away. She felt hurt by defeat. Her foolish heart failed to see breathing destructive spasms coming between her son and the typewriter. But how was a mother to know that hidden behind her cross was a Simon ready and willing to research areas where she strode as a stranger. How could she know that Eva brought service to a head and that science now was going to join forces with her. Now a new drug was being administered to the spastic boy and even though he was being allowed to take only a small segment of Lioresal tablet, he was beginning already to feel different. The little segments of Lioresal tablet seemed harmless, but yet they were the mustard seeds of his and Eva's hours of discovery.

Now he struggled from his certainty that he was going to succeed and with that certainty came a feeling of encouragement. The encouragement was absolute, just as though someone was egging him on. His belief now came from himself and he wondered how this came about. He knew that with years of defeat he should now be experiencing despair, but instead a spirit of enlightenment was telling him you're going to come through with a bow, a bow to break your chain and let out your voice.

At the very same hour fate was also at work on Eva. When it was least expected she sensed that music of which he sampled. She watched Joseph in the mirror as he struggled to find and tip the required keys. Avoiding his teacher's gaze, he struggled on trying to test himself. Glee was gambolling but he had to be sure.

Breathing a little easier, his body a little less trembling, he sat head cupped in Eva's hands. He even noticed the scent of her perfume but he didn't glance in the mirror. Perhaps it won't happen for me today he teased himself but he was wrong, desperately, delightfully wrong. Sweetness of certainty sugared his now. Yes, he could type. He could freely hit the keys and he looked in the mirror and met her eyes. Feebly he smiled but she continued to study him. Looking back into her face he tried to get her response, but turning his wheelchair she gracefully glided back along the corridor to his classroom.

Of the great discovery Nora knew not and Joseph chose not to tell her. Boyblue bested his body but he bragged but to himself.

'Mrs Meehan, have you seen Joseph at his typing?' innocently enquired Eva Fitzpatrick. 'No, Eva, he hasn't been at his typewriter for about eighteen months now,' said unwary Nora. Eva smiled in understanding but asked Nora, 'Will you come to see him at his next typing lesson?' 'Sure,' said innocent Nora, 'when do you take him again?' 'Next Wednesday afternoon at 2.15,' said Eva.

Nora sat watching. Spasms ripped through Joseph's body. Sweat stood out on his face. He was trying to let his mother see what he was capable of. She was not impressed. He could see that despite his ordeal. The phone rang and Eva suggested that perhaps Nora would take over from her and hold Joseph's head. The spasms held him rigid but within a couple of minutes he felt himself relaxing. Nora waited, her son's chin cupped in her hands. Then he stretched and brought his pointer down and typed the letter 'e'. Swinging his pointer to the right he then typed another letter, and another one and another. Eva finished speaking on the telephone and Nora, while still cupping Joseph's chin turned and said, 'Eva, I know what you're talking about – Joseph is going for the keys himself – I could actually feel him stretching for them.' Eva, his courageous teacher, clenched her fist and brought it down with a bang on the table. 'So I was right, I was afraid to say anything, I had to be sure,' she said as she broadly smiled.

Joseph sat looking at his women saviours. They chatted about their discovery while he nodded in happy unbelievable bewilderment. He felt himself float reliably on gossamer wings. He hungered no more. He giggled nervously before he even bespoked his thanks. He cheered all the way up the corridor, said goodbye to dear Eva and giggled and cheered up into Nora's face all the way home.

Feeble Joseph was just eleven years old, but before long he would be taking on Nora, schooling her to see what he could see, instructing her to steady his head for him while he typed beauty from within, beauty of secret knowledge so secretly hidden and so nearly lost forever.

It was by nodding his head then that he bashfully typed green words, frail poems and childish prose. Writing became Joseph Meehan's Word-Wold. Brain-damaged, he had for years clustered his words, certain that some Cyclops-visioned earthling would stumble on a scheme by which he could express hollyberried imaginings.

Certain of himself and his word bunting, he was confident enough to feed himself on fame. Nested writing brought him naïve belief that he could compete with other writers. Now he was waiting the results of his most recent competition.

Sensing that he might be successful in his attempts to win a prize in the Spastics Society Literary Contest, he waited. He lay in the back garden under the noonday sun. He was wondering how his breathless autobiography would fare in the literary capital of the world.

The sun bore down relentlessly, but Joseph grinned in peculiar mastery. As he looked up through strained eyes he saw seagulls soaring then diving in hungry-voiced hunting. The boy burned and grinned, teeth gritted in defiance. Tumbling yells bullied bold notions as he lay steel-jacketed by fate. Suddenly the scene heard a frantic bell. From inside the kitchen came the urgency of the telephone worrying the life out of Joseph.

Yvonne stirred suddenly, her golden tanned body jerking into life. 'I'll get it Mam,' she called as she ran up the steps to answer the telephone. Nora didn't stir, she was sitting reading the newspaper in the shade of the clothes-draped line. Sheets billowed and blew on the revolving clothesline, allowing her just a marginal amount of shade. Joseph's pale white shrunken limbs beckoned at the sun. He wanted to be tanned. He wanted to be golden just like his sister.

Yvonne ran down the steps calling, 'Mam, it's for you, it's the Spastics Society, Nina Heycock on the line.' Nora hurried inside and Yvonne followed her. Joseph lay looking up at the seagulls. He voiced defiance as they soared, wings outspread in flight – to hell with ye showing off up there, my crippled body may fly yet. Can a luckless fellow deny fate? Can he develop wings? Maybe fate will change her mind, bubble mercy, bubble nutshell-hollow beauty. But why doesn't Yvonne come back?

'Hi Joseph, you've won, you've won the Special Prize,' hollered Yvonne as she jumped down into the garden. Then throwing herself down beside her brother, she seized his hand and said, 'You lucky bugger, I'd a feeling you'd win but was afraid to tell you. I didn't want to build you up for a big let-down.' Joseph bowed and bowed at his sister. He felt just like she did but was afraid to tell anyone. Yvonne could feel the tension in his hand so she changed her tactics. 'You lucky bugger, off to London again,' she said, 'but this time don't bring me back cheap jewellery,' she advised, 'It's gold this time, or maybe silver is more suitable for my age.' Joseph burst out laughing and with the laugh came lovely temporary ease.

Yet they circled, circled, circled, those albatross-winged gulls. They flew up high then swept eyescavingly low. Joseph eyed them, but now sure of himself he scoffed in merry laughter. Nora ran back to play fairy godmother. 'He's done it again, that's the verdict from London,' she said. Joseph looked up at his seagulled scenario and craning his neck he locked his body into beauty by pressing on the ground with his heels. Now he was able to glance to the north, south, east and west and follow each gull with his eyes. 'Ah wait till you hear what the judge said, Joseph,' enthused his mother, 'They're comparing you with Joyce and Yeats and even Dylan Thomas too. Imagine. Ah, but you're very young. Very young yet.'

Joseph was very excited, very numb with happiness, very full of secret premonitions and very great gratitude. Mesmerized, he anointed vivid-voiced love. Nocturnal messages budded now, budding his withered stalk in buds of rosy-tipped shoots. He heard his mother and sister expressing their happiness for him, but he hesitated before joining them in glad-glanced mouthings. Nothing could change his crippled body but now he languished in literary shadows and he liked the view in the Market Place ahead.

Talking excitedly, Nora knelt on the ground looking into her son's eyes while Yvonne lay prone, still holding her brother's hand and snapping numb the spasms which ricocheted through his body. Her glance met his imploring glance as he directed her to his chariot. 'Mam,' she said, picking up his clue, 'Joseph wants to get back into his wheelchair.' Nora and Yvonne lifted him from the rug and eased him back into his seat. The telephone rang again, ringing ringing despite the business of the scene. 'I'll bet it's Dad,' said Yvonne as she ran again to answer it.

Nora brought Joseph's chair into the kitchen by dragging it up the two steps on its back wheels. Yvonne was chatting with her dad, telling him about Joseph's great news. Nora wheeled her son out into the dark, cold, dim hall and taking the phone from her daughter she held it to Joseph's ear. He heard his dad in mid-sentence but let out a wild cheer. Matthew stopped short and laughing said, 'Oh, it's yourself Joseph, you're a great lad. I'm very proud of you.' Then he asked, 'Are you very pleased with yourself?' But he couldn't see his son nodding furiously. Joseph glanced up at smiling Nora and indicated that it was time that she took over.

Sadness was gone out with the tide, Dollymount Strand was silent save for the family and their black and white collie dog. Restfully they strolled along the beach with Joseph now centre-stage and the *cause célèbre* for this nighttime outing. The signals flashed from the Bailey Lighthouse in Howth, challenging sailors to beware of the cased, hidden rocks. Joseph bragged to his family. He bowed and nodded towards England. They understood his signals and rejoiced for him. Even his adopted city seemed to cheer his success, for Dublin twinkled its lights in horseshoe shape around him, framing the story of Joseph Meehan in watercolours tinted with blue, green, white and gold. Water shimmered on the bay, the sound of the sea golloped his voiced thanks but he nodded towards the horizon. God, forgive me for chiding Why, he prayed, but how was a small fella like me to know that a bested prayer from me can move God to fling open the floodgates of heaven.

In the company of his family he boyishly bragged but in the silence of the night he ducked his comforter in seas of creature-cradled gratitude. Communion too brought his comforter within his grasp and in close body contact he crested silent desperate credence. Communion served grand purpose, serving to bring God to him and him to servile God.

CHAPTER SEVEN

THE NIGHT THAT WAS IN IT

F R JOHN Flynn was curate in Clontarf. Every Wednesday and Sunday he called to Joseph's house and in his inside pocket he carried the pyx bearing the consecrated bread. God assumed beautiful credit by breathing love through the eucharist. Candlelight burned as the priest began his polished prayers of terrible beauty. Then holding aloft the white host, he expressed Joseph's prayer of pleading:

> 'Lord I am not worthy to receive you,
> but only say the word and I shall be healed.'

Joseph would then attempt to open his mouth to receive communion, only to find his teeth clenched tight in vice-gripped lockjaw. His eyes would dwell lovingly on his Master, voices of reverence would seep from his soul, cable-clothed God would be before him and the boy would be still trying to coax his muscles to relax and allow him to receive his Master.

Fr Flynn soon became aware of ways and means of helping Joseph to relax his muscles. From watching the Meehan family dealing with spasms he learned that one must surprise sometimes, make a sudden move and grip Joseph's chin, while other times say something unexpected. Years of trial and error had made experts of the family. Now the great gentle priest joined forces with them in their efforts to combat Joseph's rebellious body.

Hidden cries for help nested in Joseph's pleading look. It was Yvonne especially who came to his rescue. Pretending that she didn't even notice his difficulty, she would very suddenly make her move. In a lightning-fast move she would press on his forehead with one hand whilst leaning on his chin with the other and whether as a result of her spontaneous action or his own startle reflex Joseph could then beautifully relax his jaw. Fr Flynn would nod in thoughtful credit as voicing great words of worship he'd place the white host on the boy's tongue.

The difficulty associated with opening his mouth might not happen again for many months, but now the priest was more than a match for Joseph's spasm-ridden body. An avid reader of P.G. Wodehouse, bold Fr Flynn came up with ideas of his own. Once when Joseph was in difficulty, the priest standing holding up Corpus Christi glanced knowingly at the eucharist and said, 'Hi Joseph, what were you doing in the church yesterday? Were you riflin' the poor box?' Joseph was so surprised by the accusation that his mouth fell open in astonishment. The priest immediately returned to prayer as he placed communion on Joseph's tongue. Such were his schemes, such his empathy that the boy became more and more relaxed with the passing months and years.

Baffled by beauty, slow to worry, able only to think, Joseph continued on his lively path through life. He merrily looked towards his friends, for they were sharp enough to be able to feel for him in his plight. But his friends could not be on hand all the time so he turned to radio and television for company. His radio sat beside his bed bringing him music, current affairs and great lively drama. On Sundays he heard Mass on it but when Mass was finished he tumbled in rhythm to pop music. Momentous programmes in the area of the arts oftentimes left him wishing that he could hear more and more poetry. Feasting on other people's work, he never ever imagined that he would one day hear his own poetry being read on the air.

The bleeps on the radio heralded approaching one o'clock. It was Christmas Eve and time for the news. The bulletin was entitled 'The World This Weekend'. The programme was coming from the BBC in London. Joseph sat listening to the newsreader bringing him the very latest news from all around the world. Filling in the details were their own correspondents situated in the particular country in question. As the programme neared its end, the presenter told his audience that he had four distinguished people joining him and that he had invited them to tell him 'what was the most impressive moment' for each one of them in the year now drawing to a close. Mrs Edna Healey, wife of Denis Healey, Chancellor of the Exchequer, and herself a writer, was one of his chosen guests. And to Joseph's frantic amazement she said that 'reading Joseph Meehan's poetry was the highspot of my year.' Joseph sat listening, his heart doing its best to blot out what Edna Healey was saying. She explained why she was chosen to judge his poetry in the literary contest run by the Spastics Society. The programme ended bell-ringing beauty into the young boy's Christmas when the presenter invited actor Haydn Jones to read Joseph Meehan's poem 'I Peer Through Ugliness'. Radio crunched away his isolation, and as he sat listening to that voice in London, a silence silent as Bethlehem birthed joy now, the name of which busied his heart into hesitating, messaged mesmerism.

Joseph was then twelve years old and his Christmases were now spent in Dublin, but the Christmases of his childhood were stamped indelibly in his child's mind, for though childish-notioned, they bred memories of fear as well as delight. Not able to voluntarily close his eyes and feign sleep meant that Baby Jesus took only second place to Santa Claus in Joseph's scheme of things. 'Now hurry on and get to sleep, otherwise Santa won't come,' coaxed his mother, but poor Joseph was not able to get to sleep, not able to get down under the blankets and hide, and worst of all not able to close his eyes and shut out his fear of Santa. His real fear lay in the knowledge that no mortal should lay eyes on the big-bellied, red-suited, white-bearded man. Moaning to himself he snuggled his head into his pillow but his boy's imagina-tion ran riot. Night-time in Corcloon on Christmas Eve was black, pitch black. Great bespoked sounds came from the high trees around the house. Thoughts of ghoulish spirits roaming from the cemetery across the road slimed slithering cries of fear each time that Whelehan's ass brayed his slow kolkhoz cry, as it were claiming God's deity and his own pride of name in being witness and comforter on the night that was in it.

Changing house also meant changing notions of boyhood to thoughts of manhood. Christmas now became the great remembrance of Christ's birth. The awareness and significance of this fact reveried comforting daymares in Joseph's heart:

> Christmas cheered the cheerless,
> Jasmine-freckled the frail,
> Beckoned home the blacksheep,
> Mollified heaven's pain.

December now was spent in lovely dazzly Dublin. Joseph travelled in and out of the city on the train. His dad hurtled along bringing his son all the magic and music, hullabaloo and razzmatazz of Christmas in the capital of Ireland. The crowds made way for the boy in the wheelchair, the waitresses put extra cream in his coffee, the shopkeepers beautifully looked pleased with his choice of presents, while the porters helped him board his train at the vantage point for him. For lonely youth he gave not a fig, here he was now watching people's faces, smiling at times as street dealers raucously bellowed, 'Buy your Christmas wrapping paper. . . . Lovely balloons. . . . Christmas decorations. . . . Get your fairy lights. . . . Look son, lovely Christmas crackers – last two boxes.' Never offended if passed by, they just revved up and bellowed again. Seeing but not believing, the boy loved the burly busy streets. Great chains of fairy lights mimicked magic for his lost chances. In multicolour Henry Street and back-in-time Moore Street he listened to the daughters of Molly Malone still wheeling and dealing from their barrows, 'Lovely juicy oranges. . . . Ripe bananas. . . . Buy your brussels sprouts – look mam, lovely and fresh. . . . Fresh musharooms.' Moidered by brash niceness of sounds, healed by being part of the scene, warmed by the rosy-cheeked women clutching their mugs of pure unlaced tea, he nodded to his father, hinting that his frame was filled and that it was time to move on.

Joseph always cutchied down inside his scarf as his father wheeled him across the Liffey. Glancing through the bridge balusters his eyes buttonholed glimpses of the sombre, neon-marbled looking glass beneath. Seconds away from O'Connel Bridge was

D'Olier Street. Frantic rushing traffic snaked along, but Matthew steered his bus in and out through the convoyed, belching streams. Then with a prayer and a promise, the man and boy dropped into the chapel in D'Olier Street. Theirs would be but a fleeting visit, in one door and out the other they hurried, yet taking just long enough to salute Christ in the Blessed Sacrament. Then leaving the gentle silence of the oratory behind them, they trundled around the corner at Trinity College. Joseph would busy himself glancing from the colonnaded old parliament house to the mullioned windows of the ancient university. A hasty look at Dame Street was all he ever needed – he would have his eye hurtling on towards the street of his dreams. As though not to fail him, Grafton Street always laid on burly surprises for boys bleary-chastened. Buskers rippled their music on the frosty cold air, choirs of carol singers nested the opulence of the stores in the manger at Bethlehem while goggle-eyed children asked thousands of questions to parcel-laden parents about the moving animals in Switzer's shop windows.

Joseph always loved the special feeling of suppressed excitement in glamourous Grafton Street. His face might be blue-cold but inside he would feel comfortable and cosy. He always watched and secretly examined folk as they paraded themselves up and down the fashionable street. He felt zoo-caged and wished he wasn't, but on his visits to Grafton Street he always noted that the street was but a busy cat walk where not only the beautiful people, but punks, rockers, Jesus-freaks and beggars strutted, stumbled, posed or minced, all wanting to be noticed, all searching for something. But at Christmas time the cat walk glittered and winked at the passer by, for now it carried the ordinary folk, each of them hell-bent on getting a special gift for a certain someone.

No longer a child and fearful of Father Christmas, Joseph lived and experienced the great build-up to the family festival. His sister Yvonne decorated the tree while he blinked and wished to the rhythm of the flashing bulbs. He always had a hand in the stirring of the plum pudding and saw the intricate designs iced around the snowy landscape atop the Christmas cake. But it was the turkey that gripped his imagination. He dreaded the operation on the turkey. His dread dated back to his days on the farm where he watched the turkeys gobble-gobbling their death daily nearer. He watched the blue heads of the turkey cocks grow pink first and then blush angry red as they lowered their feathery flaps to circle in tantrums around their mates. He was always frightened by the fierceness in their frowny eyes but was fascinated by what he labelled their snot. The 'snood' was but a tiny nobbledy of fleshy string which grew between their eyes but when they got in a temper, the snot became longer until it eventually was long enough to swing hither and thither. It always reminded Joseph of a crying snotty-nosed child.

Then came killing day, the day when the choicest bird was sacrificed for family consumption. Joseph and Yvonne were inquisitive and decided to watch. Music reminded the family of 'Two turtle doves/And a partridge in a pear tree,' while out in the yard Matthew held the poor turkey by the tips of the wings and the two legs, while under the handle of the rake lay the once proud head of the fiercest turkey cock. Their dad placed a foot on either side of the frozen head under the handle and pulled. The head snapped gently, the bird was dead. Matthew picked up the cock and tied his legs together. His wings fluttered a bit. Then he hung him up by the legs on a nail in the turf shed. Yvonne was feeling sick and her brother was feeling numb. Still they watched, still they wondered. They even watched the upside-down turkey trying to gently quirk alive but their dad reassured them that the turkey didn't suffer, didn't even know what was happening.

A week passed before the turkey came centre-stage again. Nora assembled lots of old newspapers. The turkey, now naked and cold, lay upon the formica-topped table. Joseph and Yvonne, curious as cats, sat near to watch Nora plunder the turkey. Avoiding their gaze, she seemed caught up between her motherly gentleness and a brutality of mind gravitating towards a morgue and its quarry.

Wielding a sharp knife Nora cut off the lonesome, guilty-looking head, then she cut off the scaled-skin legs. Next she slit the turkey open and forced the flesh to yield. She eased her hand up into the cavern. A huge gllomp sighed from the depths within.

She began to pull. The expression on her face matched the sounds from the dead. At last she pulled the innards outwards. Another resurrecting plurpp issued with the issue. She left her booty upon the newspapers. With blood upon her hands she eased her fingers down inside the throat skin and pulled until the windpipe broke. She held the ringed cord in her fingers for a moment as if measuring its length. Back down the trembling throat curled her fingers again. 'I'm trying to catch the crop,' she explained, her voice throaty with trembling. He could see her fingers bothering the breast skin. Then they ripped out the crop. It looked like a burst balloon and was inclined to twist around her fingers. Turning her attention then to the offal saturating the newspapers, she separated the liver and the blueshot purple-edged gizzard from the sluggish green guts. Parcelling the bilious remnants, she went outside to place them in the waste bin. Returning to her bloody task she picked up the heart. It had clotted blood nestling in its chambers. She dropped it into a bowl of water. Then she showed her children the gall bladder, which was attached to the liver. She explained about its green contents, and cutting away the green sac, she placed the liver in the bowl. Now she slit open the turkey's stomach. The gizzard was full of grit, corn and shale. Nora removed the contents and washed the gizzard, then she brought it back and showed the watching pair the golden wrinkled lining within the stomach muscle. Finally she carried the dismembered corps over to the sink, asked Yvonne to fetch the drum of salt and purifying the bird she left it to drain on the stainless steel sink.

Joseph couldn't sleep that lonesome night. Lonesome thoughts ruined his childhood's Christmas. What the turkey did to his childish faith in a loving mother, Santa crowned by slyly slipping down the chimney of his mind to prey upon his imagination.

But now that was all behind him. The Dublin turkey was described as 'oven-ready' and with the minimum of effort he could shut out the past and swear that the city turkey never had a life, never lost its head. The operation on the city bird was swift; in no time at all Nora had it stuffed and wrapped then in tinfoil. Her chores were many but she never complained. Time was her bogey-man, she felt it necessary to have every job completed in time for the churning noises.

Bells pealed in all the Dublin churches as midnight nudged home its bashful meaning to all the crazy longing. Christ the God-child now breathed a human breath. The Word became flesh and dwelt amongst man. Manger-cradled the Saviour lay. Midnight Mass marked the moment for Joseph; crested now with knowing, he marvelled at the nobility of the human person.

Nora cemented duty into a great festive feast on Christmas Day. Her dinner table glittered and glinted light from silverware and cut glass. Wonderful juices oozed from Joseph's gums as he watched his father carve stuffing-edged slices from the golden-breasted turkey. 'Bless us oh Lord and these thy gifts which of thy bounty we are about to receive,' prayed the family before dining but Nora, glancing around the table at her family, always added her own special prayer, an ancient Irish plea for continuation of life, 'Go mbeirimid beo ar an am seo aris'. Joseph sat at the table watching and taking part in the family's conversation. Candles burned, softly sealing the scene in his memory. Royal red wine nestled in his glass and blinked in warm cosy beckoning to his manhood. But it was the final touch that he most wanted to live through. Matthew extinguished the candles while Nora carried to the table the crack-of-breath, blue-flame-spurting plum pudding.

CHAPTER EIGHT

AN EYEFUL OF DERRAVARAGH

WITH Christmas over Joseph decided to work hard in school. His friends though had other ideas and, indeed, when he got to school each day and joined the pack, he was gradually won over to their way of thinking. Every scheme and every ploy was considered in the hope of avoiding the next class. With each passing day the gang got smarter and the plans grew cuter. But despite their best-laid plans, crass failure stalked around every corner. Smartness among students echoed notions twice as smart in the mind of their class tutor. Jim Casey foiled their best attempts, for with a rattle of his keys as they leapt on his belt, he could be heard approaching long before his wary eye sized up his nervous victims. Then putting on his judicial voice he'd enquire, 'What's going on here, why aren't you in class?

But friendships never blossom in a classroom situation and Jim Casey seemed acutely aware of that. He watched Joseph secretly nibbling his way into the hearts of his friends. He pretended he was cross but oftentimes he caught his student's eye and smiling a kindly smile, he winked a wink as if to hint that he was in full sympathy with Joseph's schoolboyish pains to cast comfort for himself.

Easter beckoned next bringing real relief at the thoughts of Peter's invitation to Loch Derravaragh. The lake of the oaks told a story all ancient, but now masked boyhood threshed excitedly at his coming sojourn there. 'Will you come for a day's fishing on Loch Derravaragh?' coaxed Joseph's friend, 'I'm going down to Multyfarnham to spend a week camping by the lake.' The boys were sitting chatting in the mall. Joseph jumped with excitement at his friend's invitation and Peter watched his eyes saluting the enquiry.

Loch Derravaragh was situated in Westmeath, the county of Joseph's grandparents. Lovely soft hills fell down to its shore. The road from Glenidan corkscrewed through those hills, giving here and there an eyeful of Derravaragh.

The day with the Nicholsons was a sample of Galilee. The boat navigated by Peter's father chattered serenely while Peter and his brother trawled for fish. The sky was overcast, rain just managed to hold off. Joseph sat among his friends and felt as one with them. Lonely days were but a dream; now he never looked back, never looked forward, never asked for tidings of joy. Now, his cup was huge and his purse was no longer empty. Life was letting him thumbsuck for comfort for now, city-festered, french-horned-boldness yelled fire in his findings. Bashfully his friends man-handled him, but more often than not, he manhandled their boyhood's greasepaint.

'Are you enjoying it?' asked Peter as he shouted into Joseph's ear, and the boy in the boat bowed blissfully, casting his eyes to heaven then for an encore. Joseph scanned the blowing waters, bellowing his joy he sang open-mouthed. The noise of the motor drowned his music but geared voices bespoke aesthetic sound.

Delight broke his heart in nested thoughts of his grandmother. He glanced across the lake towards the Crookedwood road. He clearly imagined her as a young bride being driven from her new home in Glenidan to her nearest big town, Mullingar. She'd have sat beside her husband Joseph, and would have felt the breeze blowing off the lake. She'd have glanced out here he reminded himself, but she never ever could have imagined her son's son scudding along the surface of her breezy song-filled silence. Her Model T Ford would surely have the hood down, and her eyes might now and then fill with tears at the silent musing of her folk-taled thoughts about 'The Children Of Lir.'

Gracefully gliding along, the boat basked beautifully on the crest of the swell. Excitement suddenly established all hell. Peter tried to wind in his catch but the reel unwound just as though he had caught a shark. Perch were the fresh catch that day.

Evening-time found the fishermen seated around a crimson fire. Smoke filtered the boy's dreams. Fish cooked over the red burnt sticks. Bloodless juices drained from the cooking perch. Lake-waters crept near, stealing among the rushes and stones, it seemed to trace a message then wisely wipe it away again. The smell of the grilled fish lingered in Joseph's mind but out towards the horizon, the watching eyes of the boy spotted four swans, as silently and quondam-lifed, they drifted away regally towards their historical isolation.

Back home in Clontarf he cud-chewed. He grabbed for a hold on life and plagued his friends. They never seemed to mind his heron-like wait, but like Hecuba they nudged him along all rindstoned paths. Never able to limb his hushed boyhood, he nebula-nymphed his bony hayhurdles and cradled absolute joy where tried but wearied folk breasted help.

Everything was debated in the Meehan kitchen. Holidays held pride of place in Nora's scheme of things. It was June, and time for the family to go away for a well-earned break. Numbed by work she still heeded the needs of her family where holidays were concerned. The Meehans deliberated upon whether they should choose lovely Kerry once again, or maybe they could be adventurous and choose somewhere different. The Burren in Co. Clare was mooted by Nora and the children sensed that it would be a great chance to see someplace different, and they sensed too that there was something special about the Burren.

Quietly Matthew listened while the children enthused about the caravan versus an hotel. Assessing which would give greater freedom they settled for the caravan. They knew it would involve hard work for everybody, but the thought of waking up in the morning in some strange area of Ireland to eat breakfast at leisure and plan a day's activities was something to be grabbed at. There was another reason why the pair chose a caravan holiday – they wanted to bring their big collie dog Bruce with them. They felt that a hassled dog would regain his stature by returning to the country to smell out rabbits or cock his leg in peace. As the crested holiday time approached, the family set about loading the caravan. Clothes, crockery and accoutrements were kept to a minimum. The radio, draughts and playing cards were included for fear of a wet day, but Nora had to keep her eye on Yvonne and Joseph for they would like to bring everything they owned.

The caravan bumped and jigged behind the family car as the Meehans traversed the country en route to Co. Clare. Dreams could not match the scene. Joseph was singing though nobody seemed to notice. Yvonne and her brother were in high dudgeon with excitement. His sister nudged him to look at things that caught her attention, and if he failed to turn his head quick enough, Yvonne grabbed hold of it and turned it anyhow. Joseph didn't always co-operate with her for he had his own eyes and he chose to do his own spotting and sighting. Sometimes he didn't co-operate with Yvonne, for a fella has to keep a sister at bay, so it was purely for pigiron that he chose to look the other way. He got mad with her for bullying him – after all he never tried to ram his sightings down her throat. Woeful arguments would ensue, but while his sister argued with abrasive words he held his own by screeching or giving her daggers' looks.

Seeming to be at variance, the brother and sister really got on well together. They shared natural but remembered moments from their childhood days on the farm. They now appreciated their freedom to travel and at most were great company for each other. Music made them join forces against their parents. Driving along Matthew and Nora would forever listen to news bulletins and stick-in-the-mud music, but Joseph would give a look up to heaven pleading for patience. Between them then they'd plead their case and eventually they'd finish up bopping to their favourite pop music.

Music billowed from the car radio, heavenly countryside stretched away into the distance as the family sat and enjoyed their picnic lunch. Bruce enjoyed his new freedom after his journey in the boot of the car. Now he rolled in the long grass moaning and groaning with pure pleasure. High overhead the blue sky hung not a cloud, bees buzzed in the wild woodbine, and Joseph bested a shredded salad-sandwich down into his nervously happy stomach. Then looking in all directions his family hollered, 'Fire away ya divil ya,' as a signal to him to urinate and be finished before the next car crept up on him. Sometimes he couldn't with the laughing and then they'd shout 'Woa, hold it, there's a car coming.' It was an absolute frenzy for him, but his family managed to make light of his difficulties.

Joseph Meehan was busy as a nailer on the approach to the Burren. He had been trying to imagine what was in store for him. He saw a mental landscape showing sea, sandy beach, dunes and shelter belts, but on arrival at Fanoir he found his masterpiece was sadly lacking. Matthew lifted him from the car, but before he had even settled him in his chair, the boy was garnering first impressions of the mysterious Burren. Seeing a faint flicker of light he gazed out to sea and there, nodding on the horizon, he saw a fleet of fishing boats fireflying their way to or from their fishing grounds. Matthew strapped him into his wheelchair, but not wasting a second the boy was scanning his surroundings for instant sightings.

Crepuscular light softened a great range of mountains to Joseph's right, but fresh wildness broke the spell for him. It gushed into his hearing, busying itself in his creative mind. The tumbling torrent filled him with inquisitiveness and he immediately beckoned his dad to wheel him over to the demanding stream. Matthew shook his head saying, 'Wait now, first things first. Wait till I ask permission to stop here.' Off his dad set for the nearest house and returning in a few minutes he said, 'No problem, the lady of the house said that we're welcome to stay as long as we like. We can get fresh milk down in the local shop in the morning as the owner keeps his own cows. She said too to watch for stray cattle because they knocked down someone's tent last week and destroyed everything.' But all the while Nora was working, she checked to see if Joseph was comfortable in his chair and then roping in Yvonne, she asked her daughter to unpack some delph. Matthew meanwhile rigged up the gas supply to the caravan, and Nora put the kettle on to boil over the blue jet. All hands worked except Joseph – he sat and played gaffer.

Leaving food prepared for devouring, the parents and their

grinning son set out for the mountain stream. Yvonne had already escaped and she and Bruce had been splashing up and down in the cold spring water. The family drank deeply of sounds while bubbles of loneliness stole away down under the bridge at the road and further down towards Fanoir of the golden beach.

Sackfilling his nostalgic notions for bringing back to Dublin, the young boy was anxious to go scouting the lessons of the Burren. But Nora had other ideas. Calling all together she glanced about her. 'Where's Bruce?' she enquired. Matthew whistled sharply and Bruce came blundering along. Matthew glanced at Yvonne and reminded her that she was to keep an eye on the dog. 'He must not be let wander off. Remember that,' he scolded. The beautiful stone-floored stream begged further inspection but Nora was spoiling everything for curious Joseph. 'Come on supper's ready. Tomorrow is another day,' insisted his mother, and Matthew weary after the long drive joined his wife in her efforts to curb their children's curiosity. A tired family settled down for the night.

Matthew tied Bruce to the drawbar of the caravan, but the dog chose to sleep underneath it for shelter and company. As sleep was slow in coming, all the family chatted about what they had seen. Talk centred around the barrenness of the place. Matthew and Nora filled in the history of the area. The children learnt that the Burren was a limestone plateau and that it must once have been a tropical seafloor. They tried to imagine the disturbance in nature which hundreds of millions of years ago drove the seafloor upwards. Their parents told them that on the morrow they could see for themselves what the iceage accomplished in the Burren.

As the parents explained the mystery of the area, Joseph lay listening. Yvonne was asking the questions but eventually Matthew demanded her silence. 'Ssh,' he said, 'get some sleep now, otherwise we'll be too tired tomorrow to go exploring.'

In the narrow bunk beds Joseph could find nowhere to leave his out-stretched arms. His hand banged against the windowpane, against the caravan side even against the built-in wardrobe which was situated up behind his head. 'Ssh, keep your hands quiet, I can't sleep,' ordered Yvonne. Joseph complained in his fashion but his hand still beat out its tom-tom rhythm. Yvonne then decided to keep him awake too and so she chatted to him about Bruce, about his sitting in the boot of the car that day in Gort, defending himself by growling, while rows of frenzied dog's eyes glared in at him through the space in the slightly open boot. 'Did you see how brave Bruce was in his own car', laughed Yvonne, 'and did you notice, Joseph, how high the dogs were when they couldn't get at him?' Such was the chat until Joseph relaxed and hearing her brother give big long yawns, Yvonne faded herself out too.

Each step sounded scratchy on the tin roof but Joseph's eyes popped in his head when he saw the beady-eye of the crow side-eyeing down at him through the skylight in the roof. Yvonne woke too and lay very still looking up at the visitor. Just then Joseph's kinky hand moved and the black bird hurried away desperate in fright.

Growls growled, low-keyed, beneath the caravan, breaking in again on the silence of the new morning. Snarls frenzied Bruce's bone-lazy nodding as alert now he guarded his family. Really awake now, Matthew sat up in bed and fingering back the curtain he looked out. He jumped from his bed saying, 'here come the cattle,' and hurrying out, he chased away the full-belly-tricks, hising cattle. That done he connected the gas cylinder and came inside to cook breakfast for his clan. But everybody was now awake and Yvonne sat up to investigate her surroundings. Voicing delight she cried, 'Oh Joseph, you should see what I see. There's islands just over from us. Look Dad, what islands are they? Lift Joseph up till he sees them.' Matthew joined the children and looking out he said, 'They're the Aran Islands.' Lifting his son then, he supported him in a sitting position while the young boy looked all about the scene. Joseph was never more happy as he sat glancing hither and thither. The early morning sun glinted off the calm blue sea, the thatched whitewashed cottages nestled in rest, birds flew high in an azure dome while the delph-painted islands beckoned a welcome to a crippled cousin. Nora sat up, looked out, yawned playfully and lay down again. She knew the rules too well to disturb herself. Matthew fried breakfast, made porridge for Joseph and made lots of golden toast for Yvonne. Such were the rules. Nora got breakfast in bed while on holidays. Yvonne cashed in on the arrangements and bubbling over with happiness she chatted, sang and gregged her brother about his not being able to eat toast in bed. But his happiness knew no bounds either. He helped himself to food of a different kind. He relished family membership which always included him in utopia-linked, handicapped but natural frolics.

Certain chores had to be done and then the family moved over to the mountain stream. They washed and splashed but as ever Joseph was there too. Nora lifting him from his chair handed him to Matthew. Barefooted he was let splash, let feel the wild, surging, frantic-flowing water, let stand on the hard, cold, rock floor, and curl his toes and see how white and graceful looked his feet under the spring-cool water. As he sampled watery delights his eye fell downstream towards the stone bridge, and looking back up into his dad's face and catching his eye, Joseph indicated the bridge. Lifting his son higher, the pair set off towards the tunnel under the road. Yvonne hurried after them. She was sharptoned because Joseph had upstaged her. Yes, hyacinth-blue the sky and hyacinth-sweet the scent which wafted on the air that morning. Fanoir could boast of much more than a golden beach.

Each day brought new discoveries. Away through silent rock tomes the Meehans wandered, Joseph sitting perched on his father's shoulders, Yvonne and Bruce bounding ahead while Nora stayed near drawing her son's attention to wild flowers, the likes of which he had never seen before. 'Come 'ere till you see where this flower grows,' called Nora and together father and son looked down into a narrow crevice between the cut stone slabs and saw the sapphire-blue gentian nestling in beautiful isolation. Gazing around him from his high altitude, the boy noticed too how desperate was the plight of the trees in the barren Burren. They grew among the great rock tomes, scalded by the reflected sun and swept into stunted frozen shape by the brazen winds, yet they clung on as though they were trying to walk their message into terrafirma's slate.

Rambling through glistening orchids, gentians, meadowsweet

and wild rock roses cloned from breezeblown, bird-couriered seed, the family stepped on scattered floral carpets strewn here and there among the rocks. Joseph festered hymns of wonder at beauty born from limestone. He rode his human beast of burden and gazed down into wells of verdant flower-cushioned greenery. Suddenly Yvonne called Bruce's attention to a fleetfooted hare and sadly flatfooted the poor dog obliged and started off with great determination to catch his quarry. The hare streaked away, while Bruce, disorientated now, ran this way and that trying to pick up the scent. Then, as if deciding that following hares was beneath a collie's fashion, he lay down and laughed, his ham-pink tongue lollying in terrible exhaustion.

Each day the weary family finished their adventures by going for a swim. Fanoir of the golden beach asked for company; not a soul frequented the sea. The lingering sun gashed the evening sky in colours of red, burnt ochre, golden orange and turquoise blue. Matthew togged first in readiness to take Joseph, and then Nora and Yvonne joined them in the billowing Atlantic Ocean. Between them then all hands joined forces to help Joseph swim and float in the warm currents. They floated him with them as they moved out to sea; he glowed with pleasure as he skimmed along, for he felt totally relaxed and safe in their hands and through their efforts he sampled the joys of the able-bodied.

Upon returning to the beach one evening the family designed another treat. They burrowed a hole deep down into the fine sand and when it was deep enough they sowed Joseph and filled in the sand around his body. Only his head and shoulders remained above ground. They tramped the sand firmly about him and then stood back to see him standing on his own two feet. Bruce circled round him barking in bewilderment. Joseph desperately freckled his scene with questions. Is this how the world should be he wondered. He gazed out to sea and watching the soft greased waves creeping ever towards him, he grimaced at the horizon. Freed now, he frescoed farsighted fame. Looking around him he was monarch of all he surveyed but master of none. He looked at feet instead of faces, he looked at slanting sun dimming boy's fun. His feet hinted that they only nursed boots, his legs told bold hurt and his body budged to get back to normality. Bruce had to be called off by Yvonne, she raced away calling on the dog to come follow her and allow his friend to enjoy his beggared independence. But the longer he stood the more he learnt. Now his mind was establishing lonely thoughts and lonely longings. Looking back out to sea he gadded along the horizon. He was silently distancing himself from doleful, shame-filled yearning. As he scanned his lonesome life he knew his chair was his throne, his feet were but his companions. He watched his chance and catching his father's eye he indicated that he wanted to get back to his grand wheelchair. Matthew began to scoop back the fine sand. The golden light seemed to filter through his fingers. Joseph was now wobbling like a reed in a storm. Nora leapt into action and clutched a hold on his swaying body. Now he was almost free. Nora clutched a tighter hold of her son and now she lifted him higher and hither. He felt his feet slither from their grave. Matthew held out his hands to take his son's sand-sprayed body. Then cradling him in his arms he carried him towards a big towel which lay on a patch of grass. As he lightly brushed the sand from his boy's body, he said, 'Did I ever tell you about the walrus and the carpenter?' He didn't even look for a response from Joseph, he was off with his recitation:

> The Walrus and the Carpenter
> Were walking close at hand;
> They wept like anything to see
> Such quantities of sand:
> 'If this were only cleared away,'
> They said, 'it would be grand!'
>
> 'If seven maids with seven mops
> Swept it for half a year,
> Do you suppose,' the Walrus said,
> 'That they could get it clear?'
> 'I doubt it,' said the Carpenter,
> And shed a bitter tear.

Fun-filling each day of the holidays gave great happiness to Matthew and Nora. They cooked light meals and brought picnics to have out among the mountains of the Burren. The wheelchair was no help at all for the rocky terrain ruled out its usefulness, but undeterred the Meehans wandered, Joseph riding high on his dad's shoulders while Nora carried the foodstuffs. Fresh air breasted their strength as higher and higher they climbed amidst the huge rocks. Resting for lunch on the slabs they chatted about freedom, freedom to be really in tune with nature. The family talked, listened to the sound of absolute silence, unctioned their tired bodies and cradled their needy one. Joseph basked in the wonder of it all, he soaked in the conversation but all the while his eyes roamed and wandered.

Attracted by the sudden sound of pattering feet, Joseph's attention was drawn one afternoon to a huge pillar overshadowing the picnic setting. Turning swiftly he saw an ancient bearded face peeping around the great stone. The saucer-sized eyes were staring at Bruce, but poor foolish dog that he was, he detected nothing as he lay smiling in ignorance. The buff-coloured puck goat emerged to face the scene, four feet set firm in defiance while goggle-eyed nannies and kids skipped and bleated in scared disarray. A heavy pungent odour wafted on the air. Gloated goat that he was, he seemed to object to hillbillies intruding onto his ancient stony fortress. Bruce, now on his feet, barked and barked, whether from desire to guard his family or (bastard that he was) maybe he was jealous of geared fraternal numbers among the goat herd. The natural owners disturbed the family resting place, so they decided then to move on.

A dolmen silhouetted against the evening sky linked the dead past with the loitering now. The tired child-bearer slid his son from his shoulders and placed him on the headstone to rest. Nora, taking over, put her son in a sitting position so as to allow him to view his surroundings from a natural stance. Feeling more independent now, the boy sat relaxed. Death lay cold in the grave beneath him and secretly he exchanged regards with silent frescoed forefathers. Fashioned grave that it was, the dolmen stamped the message of time on this timeless land.

Ferreting for unique experiences, varnished joys and frank certainties vested Joseph and his family with a purpose and reason for living. They created humble life, but for Joseph it was never humble at all. The holiday in Clare served to wake his senses, give resolve to his ambitions, secrete his desires and desiccate his feelings of frustration. Thus he sat in silence, his family all the while working, but his youthful boy's mind was recording a final landscaped look at the Burren. Dour grey mountains reared in yew-drossed bunting, fern fossiled crude stone, time oozed from lunar landscaped barrenness while a rushing stream seeded life, desperate as it was to loom a thread by which a fellow might knit a name worth tuppence.

Return journeys assume an air of anticlimax always, but on his return journey to Dublin the boy was trying to cradle his casts of stone bindweed while in his future London was calling westward again for waddling mundane boy Joseph Meehan.

CHAPTER 9

IF HE COULD BUT EARTH HIMSELF

H AVING won the Special Prize for the second time, Joseph was relaxed on the flight to London. It wasn't a case of *déjà vu*, but unlike the first trip he was able to conquer his fears this time. He felt truly relaxed in the atmosphere created by the British Spastics Society, so now he was really looking forward to meeting grand friends. True to their service, everything was laid on for their prizewinner from Ireland. Bonded hope flowed from their generosity answering a need for solace in the awful hassled existence of every brain-damaged person. Their thoughtfulness could be measured restfully through all their royal preparations. Resurrecting a cripple from the status of beggar birthed their every forethought. Seeing that the flight didn't get into Heathrow Airport until 8.30pm, Aer Lingus mobilized special transport for their native son and with great astuteness they whisked Joseph and Nora to Fitzroy Square, for it was there that the Literary Contest organizers now waited. As on the previous occasion, cold supper was left in readiness and once sure that the Meehans were beautifully welcomed, they slipped away to allow Joseph to sup in peace and privacy.

The Literary Luncheon next day was a lovely relaxed affair. Catering staff seemed at ease as they served and attended to the physically handicapped guests. Joseph sat watching; he always chose to dine alone for the mere matter of swallowing was for him a delicate undertaking.

The prizegiving ceremony though was a different matter entirely. Joseph Meehan sat among the winners as though born for glory. He, yes, Boyblue was going to blow his horn! Under the impression that the names were going to be called in alphabetical order, he jumped when the name Joseph Meehan rang out. He swiftly glanced at the row of judges and wondered what his judge would say to him. But he had to halt his musing for Lady Georgina Coleridge herself was walking towards him. His head fell backwards as he gazed up into her face but she bent slightly in order to look him straight on. In the meantime Nora had tilted his head just slightly forward and leaving the tips of her fingers as a headrest she enabled him to face his judge from a normal head position. 'Joseph,' she said, 'congratulations on your excellent winning entry,' and then smiling warmly she went on, 'You have promise, your writing has touches of Joyce and even traces of the Welsh poet Dylan Thomas.' Presenting him with the large white envelope containing his award, Lady Georgina insisted, 'You must go on writing. You have real talent.' Joseph smiled sheepishly and bowed rapidly. He was hoping to convey his youthful respect of her desire to encourage him. With a purposeful handshake she moved back to her seat in order to allow the next judge to deliver his prize. Feeling numbed with joy and happiness, Joseph scanned her face. Yes, no doubt in the world, that lady meant what she said.

As was his custom, Joseph now swam free from his strangled body. He could feel the closeted, cossetted certainty of Christ calming his soul and questioning, 'Why are you fearful – see how the spirit moves.' Tears knocked but he blinked and determined not now. Consciously he tuned in to listen and share the triumph of others, but the numbing balmed his passion. Joseph however stood his ground and bowed and bowed. Had he a voice he would have bellowed and bellowed from plumbed depths of happiness.

Vast notoriety now basted the heart of Joseph Meehan. Britain jousted his disability just as fairly as though he were British-born. Beaded now as a boy genius, he figured in a great pictorial magazine published by the *Sunday Times* newspaper. Commissioned by the historically famous paper, Lord Snowdon, Britain's famed photographer, flew to Dublin to photograph Joseph sitting at his ease outside William Chambers' architectural gem, the folly known to Dubliners as Marino Casino.

Boldly he smiled from the pages of the magazine. Trapped silent for most of his short life, he spoke now not only to folk in Britain, but through this newspaper he was ferreting into the loam of countries all around the world.

Hope flowed from readers' response to the magazine article; they sensed a bold discovery and now fresh ideas were a-stir. Experts in the field of neuro-study and linguistics were delving into Joseph's writing and dumbness. Looking for traces of grim struggle, they delved. Trying to think for them Joseph worried ... will they be able to gauge my terrible struggle, he wondered, can any sane, able-bodied person sense how it feels to have evil-intentioned limbs constantly making a mockery of you. Berating himself still more he set himself another conundrum – how can even the greatest expert rescue truth from your meagre writings, after all it's when you seem asleep that you're really thinking; game but really unable, harassed but not cheated, joyful but fractured, notorious but cowardly, man but still boy, boy-writer by birth but garnered in difficulty, yessed by daffodil moments but fated in dull colours, typhooned in dolorous landscape but not abandoned, hurt but desperate to survive; and stranger still, how can they hear your cry for life, your wish to be given a chance to look out on a world where heretofore your crippled brothers ebbed away on muttonfat crosses, where sun burnt passions and melted human hearts. But Joseph voiced boy's fears, he underestimated the power of the adult intellect. The experts sable-coated him by heaping understanding on his ribald rantings.

The *Sunday Times* feature caught the attention of computer scientists and true to their calling they scanned the woeful wilderness which surrounded the disabled, voiceless boy, Joseph Meehan. Can micro-technology blast him from his strait-jacket, wondered Edinburgh University's Research Fellow, Phil Odor. Giving the matter great thought scientifically, he felt convinced that within computer science lay the grand solution to disabled man's numbness. With all the promise of an unequalled creator he came to Dublin, and devoting hour after hour to sizing up his brain-damaged student, he almightily created wonderful avenues of escape for this dumb, nodding-head boy. Quiet, devoted, he got to understand Joseph's dedication to re-writing the saga of helpless, crippled man, rejected by society and suspended in time, and to all intents and purposes seen to be waiting listlessly for the call to even greater oblivion. Used to describing his science in terms of being able to replace man's labours by the operation of one switch, Phil now found two strong hands able to do what a computer failed to accomplish. What have human hands got that a machine can't have, wondered the Research Fellow, and when Joseph rests his chin in Nora's cupped hands, what does that do for him, he mused. Joseph could have told him those two hands stream my head, as a pivot one moment, as a lift when I need to stretch forward, as a surefire suppressor of destructive lightning-fast electric charges, as a support when I'm just thinking. As hesitance marks most of my attempts to strike a letter, those hands wait and sensitively feeling the washed-up power, they hold my head until the spasm has wasted itself.

How can a mere switch consciously feel and help wasted limbs to act on command, pondered the caring expert, and watching for even one voluntary movement in Joseph's crass body, he set about harnessing that reliable bow of his head. Phil walked by Dublin Bay at night tossing in his mind the bedamned needs of Joseph Meehan. Weary from long hours glaring at the bright green glow from the computer, he fought on with his baffling research. Joseph watched and wondered, honest he said, can you believe that this big, cruel world can bring mastery plus generosity together in one man?

Such were the polarizing problems. The scientist reasoned that the greatness of technology sadly fell far short of Joseph's needs. Truly he pondered and grimly he worked, writing programmed menus which hotly held fierce hope for Joseph. With the alphabet upon the screen and the cursor hopping along from one letter to the next, all Joseph had to do now was strike his chin against a nearly placed switch and miracle of miracles, the letter would appear in a boxed-off area of the screen. There and then disability would be conquered. Conscious of the greatness in that movement by which he struck the chin-switch, Joseph waited for the green cursor to come to the required letter, but by that time his acute mind had foreseen the difficulty, his entire body froze rigid, and his eyes watched the cursor hop by. 'Don't worry, Joseph, you'll get it the next time,' counselled Phil, as he felt for the frustration of the boy. The next time was the same and the next. Quietly Phil took Joseph's hand and paced him: 'Not yet, not yet,' he whispered as he felt the iron tension building in the youth's limbs 'Not yet, not yet, be getting ready – Now' and Joseph made a wallop at the switch which almost beheaded him. Phil smiled, 'Great, great lad,' he said as he smiled in delight. With the reassurance of the human hand pacing him, Joseph managed to spell his own name.

As the *Sunday Times* was by then cognizant of disabled Joseph Meehan's plight, they became interested in not just his talent, they now put noteworthy attention on this boy's attempt to shake free from his tackle. In a follow-up feature they told of the boy's brain-damaged attempt to gain independence and the paper asked for funds to allow Joseph to purchase his own computer. Readers responded so magnificently that all in all Joseph was offered complete micro-computer units, software equipment and thousands upon thousands of pounds. The great response to the appeal stirred the young boy to his very depths. Can I, he pondered, crippled as I am, spearhead a new drive to highlight the communicative needs of tongue-tied but normal-notioned man? silently he mulled over his aspirations – if computer science can give me a voice, then everyone else who is similarly afflicted stands a chance of being freed. If I fail to make fantastic headway so be it, maybe someone just a little less constrained can bridge the gap and then certain scientific advancement will aspire to heights as yet aligned with divine pursuits. As Joseph echoed his decision to Nora and Matthew they echoed for him expectations as diverse as descried feelings, descried framework, and descried prophecies. He descried plans for a trust fund to be set up with *Sunday Times* readers' fond contributions, by which he sought to head-first a call to scientists to bring to fruition an as yet trestle-dead dream, to find a voice for the voiceless.

Certain delineations made their trembling appearance on paper as Yvonne artistically interpreted his vision. 'Might this say what you wish for yourself and fellas like you?' she asked time and time again. Joseph had an idea and feared that she might get fed up trying to meet his needs. Then with a blast of excitement he saw her line out the exact image he held, a skull in silhouette contained within a key head and right in the brain she sited the keyhole. Thus the logo was designed as birthing a daring research fund which would perhaps one day unlock the intelligence imprisoned within the crippled mute person. Yes yes yes, signalled Joseph as Yvonne put the finishing touches to the design and giving a smile of sisterly hope she said, 'Heave a sigh there lad, you worked just as hard as me.' Joseph did smile and sigh with gratitude, for harassed himself, he silently harassed anybody gullible enough to yes his busy demanding brain.

Fastening honesty onto every annex open to him, Joseph anchored his noble boy's name to a dedicated group of academics seeking to nab hold of intelligence lying dormant within disabled people. Yelling babbled findings he rejoiced threshingly, for now he saw for himself that great gaps were going to be bridged and very likely mankind, wacky-looking, was going to be no longer frowned upon.

Despite all hope, Joseph lay in his bed at night worrying and wondering. He was mesmerized by the promise within technology. Old sufferings would never again be silently momented by speechless man, now great men were busy wrangling popular thesis around yelling joy in brain-damaged man's budding rescue. Joseph thought about his research. The freedom to move muscles voluntarily was denied him; he asked movement but all he ever got was busy, jerky, muffled movement. Hands that could involuntarily give knock-out blows to anyone or anything near, became stiff and hesitant on being given a brain command. Similarly, when he tried to give a sideway flick of his chin to the switch for his computer, he found the effort exaggerated to mountainous proportions, so much so that his whole body had to gear itself in readiness to give what should have been but a slight flick of his head. Then as if that war was not great enough, he still found another cruel threat confronting him. He couldn't ever determine the precise moment at which to attempt the flick of his head. He was used to fouling-up his moment of anticipation when about to receive communion; he could wildly open his mouth when the priest entered his room or he could open it while the priest was saying the preparatory prayers, but by the time he needed to open his mouth to receive the host, his moment had passed and only sad desperation remained. So busy thinking was he that he jumped with fright, he nearly forgot his success at switching on and switching off his radio. But battles latent waited. He had to teach his muscles how to cram power into just one local movement and he had to try to find a way to anticipate the moment when he must nominate his 'go' signal. Seeing his needs didn't mean he could solve his dilemma, but he dreamt nonetheless. Gushing breath now gunfired boy's creative surrealism but he, green-fresh in writing territory, needed a ready outlet for his now bursting creations. Looking at freckled fate and looking too through Phil Odor's researching light, Joseph now knew that he could be an independent writer if he could but earth himself.

CHAPTER 10

MY BOYHOOD EPIPHANY

Not able to share his hopes or worries with others meant that school was separate from his research at home. In fairness though, there was more than enough going on in school to keep his mind occupied. Each year Mount Temple staged a musical. Colin Mackenzie produced it while his wife Patricia supported him by not alone being the pianist, but she worked mightily coaching and teaching the students about voice projection and acting. The whole staff joined in towards the end and between them all, they managed to shape awkward students into beautiful strolling players.

Joseph Meehan had never been on a stage in his life, after all who could feel that a dumb cripple could possibly want the experience, or who could be imaginative enough to invite frescoed dumbness to share the vocal arena of the very normal. But that is what happened in great-hearted Mount Temple.

'Will you be able to take part in our musical?' asked Mr Mackenzie. 'You can be in the chorus Joseph, and there'll be lots to keep you company. I'll leave it to yourself,' he said, 'but I think you should, you'd love it.' Joseph's heart done a somersault and looking into his teacher's eyes he smiled and glanced up to heaven, giving him his affirmative signal over and over again.

At around one o'clock every day Mr Medlycott came on the air to announce: 'Will all students taking part in the musical please report to the gym at two o'clock for rehearsals.' As though responding to the call of the Pied Piper, at two o'clock students could be seen pouring from different doors, all heading in dribs and drabs for the singing practice. The students were for the most part familiar with the music from *Joseph And His Amazing Technicolour Dreamcoat*, but now they had to learn the lyrics. Each day though brought decided familiarity, as pupils sang the numbers over and over again. Practice would go on all afternoon and well into the evening, but with each passing day came sureness and confidence. Joseph sat and watched, he pitied his friends as they had to go through the forge, being shaped as they were for the roles of Joseph, Jacob and Pharaoh. The dancers were screened so that nobody would distract them or mock their efforts, but great guffaws could be heard as folk with two left feet were turned into Pharaoh's skilful dancers.

By the first dress rehearsal the cast had now become almost professional. The costumes seemed to give confidence to the members. Joseph fretted for his friends; he knew their lines, he knew their songs, but he knew not their nerves. He watched as Peter Nicholson put showers of talcum powder into his fair hair, thereby adding the years for his part as Jacob. Tony Mullins wound a white sheet sarong-fashion around him, while Joseph Meehan's white robe hung over himself as well as his wheelchair and on his head he wore a large white kerchief which was held in place by a red 'iqal'. Players looked the part, as with their make-up on they were now almost unrecognizable. The atmosphere in the cloakroom was electric and bedlam reigned. But near curtain-up time teachers eventually freezed the nerves and the students lined up to take their respective entrances on stage. Tony Mullins whispered, 'Don't worry about your veil, Joseph,' as fixing his own for the last time, he then settled Joseph's prior to setting off. But no sooner on his way with the wheelchair than some clumsy foot stepped on the tail of Tony's sheet and it started to unwind. 'Great god you can't let that happen before the audience,' said cloakroom-hand and dresser for the night, Dorothy Siney, as ready for all emergencies, the teacher produced a large safety pin and laughing comradely she secured Tony's robe.

Solo musicians gave opening recitals and then it was time for the main event of the night – the Mount Temple Students' presentation of *Joseph And His Amazing Technicolour Dreamcoat*.

The curtain went up. The keen audience stretched their necks. Parents looked for their own child in the huge cast. With a sweep of his baton, the conductor breathed action and there and then unfolded a great song-filled story. 'Way, way back many centuries ago,' sang the assembled choir as they told the biblical saga of Joseph and his eleven brothers. Joseph Meehan mouthed the lovely songs, music swept him along, Tony stood beside him and down there among the blurred audience he could imagine the faces of Nora and Matthew.

The atmosphere was secretive. The story was about jealousy emerald-green, and cowardice, cowardice as yellow as a duck's foot. Joseph Meehan mouthed his namesake's fear as in biblical fresco the brothers realized that the favourite son wore the 'coat of many colours'. The audience reacted with thunderous applause and long piercing whistles. The music was intoxicating and the theme of forgiveness was evidenced when biblical Joseph forgave his now hungry and grovelling brothers. Everyone rejoiced when poor old Jacob was reunited with his son. Encores were demanded when the final curtain fell, but after allowing two repeats Mr Mackenzie cast aside any further demands, for his cast had tried very hard to do justice to the famous drama. Quietly then the students turned from the stage. Tony wheeled Joseph out into the passageway. Joseph felt the sweat grow cold on his forehead, his back too was damp with sweat. It had been a mammoth undertaking for him, but it was worth every bit of effort. He had managed to keep his arms quiet, his feet had stayed still and his mouth had framed words, beautiful words, soundless words, words savaged by broken dreams.

Celebrations in dramatic historical garb were of the stuff of school, but at home drama was all the time in the making. Joseph Meehan's breakthrough into creative territory caught the imagination of correspondents around the world. The telephone rang constantly while Joseph's family fretted certainly. The Meehans asked no quarter, but equally they gave no quarter either. They handled Joseph's handicap as though they found it normal. They used their commonsense and done away with the sob-storied views of the past. Journalists soon became aware of the family's no-nonsense attitude and being the imaginative people that they were, they tuned in quickly to the situation. They learned how to regard the handicap in relation to the boy and his creative gifts. They constantly asked him why his writing was so sparse and brief. They wondered too at his staccatoed style. Sometimes he invited them to watch him writing and sometimes he even suggested that they cup his chin in their own hands in order that they could feel the undercurrents of electricity running and molesting his attempts to strike a letter. Only thus could he convey his briefness in language, only thus could he explain why his rhythm of sound was jumpy and jarring on the ear.

The BBC radio produced a documentary about the young disabled boy and his writing. They created their story around himself, his family, his school and his writing. Poets usually read their own poetry, but in the radio documentary the producer had to engage an actor to give voice to the poetic thoughts of boy-writer Joseph Meehan.

Joseph sat watching how his story fared at the hands of the media. As he watched he saw graciousness, delicacy, fairness and faithfulness coming through the features and articles about him. He was wary of being exploited and silently kept his weather-eye upon all and sundry. The idea of foraging for himself was always to the fore of his mind. He wanted to have his fool's findings published and had a secret vision of a book of poetry by Joseph Meehan standing by itself on a shelf in his study.

Calling his mother to sit down in front of him, he got to work with his eyes. He conveyed to her that he wished to talk about himself. She nodded and with a broad grin said, 'What's new?' He dismissed her barb and became serious in his expression. He nodded towards the telephone. He beckoned her with his eyes to wheel him into his study. He bowed towards his writings and then towards the books on his shelf. All of his clues served to build up his request to have her telephone the publisher in London for him. Frowning with worry, she tried to back away from granting his request. 'Ah, don't ask me to phone him for you,' she begged. 'I wouldn't know what to say. Anyhow,' she continued, 'what'll you do if he tells you to get lost, that your writing isn't good enough or that nobody would be interested in it?' He laughed but begged her to phone by nodding and nodding at it. She floundered in the face of her son's cruel demand. She, haughty in her looks, declared, 'I haven't got his telephone number anyhow.' But coping with breathtaking difficulty was her stuff of service since her son was crassly babied near doom. Now he saw her get the telephone directory and forage through it, then putting it away she went on with her housework. Alert to her ways, he detected that she had found the number she required in order to trace the telephone number of the British publisher. Bestowing belief in her son's writings, she was now mentally schooling herself to find suitable words to make a young boy's questioning relevant to a great and fame-filled publisher.

Joseph was certain that his mother was going to do as he asked; he heard her on the phone tracing the number she required, but on returning to the kitchen she just continued with her work. He felt sorry for her but he was determined to handle his secret ambition to have his writings published. Then, suddenly, she stopped her dinner preparations and as though her thinking was sufficient unto her needs, she frowned at him and taking hold of the handles of his chair she wheeled him out into the hall. 'Remember lad, you asked for this, so be prepared for anything that comes from this call,' she cautioned and so saying she picked up the telephone and dialled the number. Joseph's eyes dwelt upon this nursed messenger of his but when his mother was finished speaking her eyes told him all he wished to know. Already familiar with Joseph's name, the London publisher lit a quiet flame of hope in the silent boy's heart when he asked to see the remainder of his writings.

At the dot of 1.15pm each day Nora always drove slowly into the schoolyard. In among all the to-ing and fro-ing she would spot her son as he, in the company of either girls or boys, made his way out to meet her. The students now familiar with Joseph's communication were fit to tease and embarrass him before his mother. She, though, familiar beyond the ordinary, was only too aware of the go-boy that nestled within his simple looking face and frame. With an air of being shocked at his classmates' revelations she encouraged them to tell her more. They, fearful of getting him into trouble, closed up abruptly and with great aplomb would change the subject and move on to safer territory. Thanking his friends, Nora would wheel him into the school, into the small room next door to Jack Heaslip's guidance room. Once there she would sit down, and while pouring out the sweet tea from the flask would fill him in on the morning's happenings at home. If there was mail for him she showed him that and then holding his head steady she would ease the tea down into his stomach.

Now it's Tuesday counted Joseph, and it was Thursday when we posted the package to the publishers. With silent scanning he was assessing his chances of Nora having a letter for him. But when she arrived at lunchtime he looked in the bag to see if there was any sign of an envelope, but only the red tartan pattern of his flask showed. He looked up into her face but it was just blank. He detected nothing in her manner and as she slowly wheeled him along the purple corridor she chatted about the fact that not only had the postman no letters, but she didn't even have a sighting of him. Opening the door of the mall, she wheeled him in to the cosy room. He watched as she poured the amber tea. Now he could wet his whistle and never fear, he could do with a visit to the toilet. Slowly she poured and then sort of casual she said, 'I had a telephone call from Weidenfeld's. "Yes, we're interested,"' they said, 'in fact they told me to tell you that they feel privileged to have been allowed to read your work and they would be honoured to publish it.' Joseph's whole body reacted, his face looked stunned, his eyes flew heavenwards, a very silence basked round his heart. He searched for a voice to utter words which his mouth framed. His body assumed the beauty of normality while his heavy cross lifted lightly from his slight back. His mother coldly dimmed from vision and his very soul was pulsating with great joy. Nora stayed silent just quietly smiling, watching. She wanted to free her son from her. Now this was his moment of birth, now he had defeated dyed death and bestowed birth to himself. He birthed an author. Slowly he moved back to reality and certainly thanked Nora for her spadework. She, just typical of the bean a ti* that she was, seemed more interested in slipping the sweet tea down into his churning stomach. That now accomplished, she thumped him on the back and said, 'Well done lad, that was marvellous news today. Don't let it go to your head though, you still have a long hard fight ahead but you're well suited for the challenge. Today you have crossed the first hurdle. Imagine what Dad and Yvonne are going to say when they hear your news. We must get Yvonne to come home for this weekend and we'll have a celebration, 'cause it's not every day that a family has so much to celebrate.' Joseph listened all the while and nodded and nodded in agreement, after all he was too numbed to certify otherwise. Fossilized for so long now, he was going to speak to anyone interested enough to listen. As was customary, far into the future he bent his mind, what will erstwhile readers think, he wondered, of my boyhood epiphany.

Feeling happy beyond words, he listened to his teachers all afternoon. They veiled their private worlds by choice, but his private world was so private that demon despair dallied always at his door. Now he cackled to himself, for now he shared the same world as everyone else; he could choose how much to tell and craftily decide how much to hold back. His voice would be his written word.

Unlike nights of old, cried cries of chilling despair now became cosy calm as the fourteen-year-old caught casked courage to his chest and asked sin's-of-doubt's forgiveness. Suds of shame seeped from his eyes as he lay on his night-sampan and slowly his bygones slipped away. Plagued Nora had more than made up to him for being the immune child that he was. Lost life nebulous-nomed him now windowed-wisdom breathed gutsy, desert-dry facts. This birthed dessert of bubbling beauty now breast-filled Joseph. Casual friends were delighted for him for the credence to which this book would lay claim. Credence assumed truth, and truth frantically followed gamely on his heels, for full service first comes from grass-green truth.

*housewife.

CHAPTER ELEVEN

I'VE CRACKED IT

S CHOOL students in Mount Temple were divided into a number of forms usually of mixed ability, boys and girls, and each form assumed a letter belonging to the word Dublin. Year by year the lettered classes changed pupils. Boys and girls had to change about in order to pursue different subjects. It so happened that Joseph's friends found themselves separated from their mate. It was September, the start of the school year, and Form 3L found Joseph on his own among a class of strangers. Everyone knew him – he was crippled gombeen-boy Joseph Meehan – but not bashful to the point of staying hidden, he now could claim genuine friends in school.

Form 3L offered a challenge to him. He now had to communicate with new boys and girls in this class. So he made his first move. He glanced hither and thither. He caught someone's eye, but they looked away. He caught someone else's eye and bowed his staccato bow at them, they gave him a hard look and then feigned interest in what Mr Casey was teaching. He tried again and again; boys and girls silently dismissed him. Schooling himself not to be easily offended, he didn't blame them – after all if he was in their shoes he'd likely act the same or even worse. Maybe he'd indicate his displeasure with a sneaky two-fingered sign! He chortled to himself and not heeding Jim Casey's explanation of assonance he tried again. Janey, I'm in luck, he mused as he caught the eye of the boy at the next desk. Joseph bowed at him and tried to smile naturally. The boy smiled briefly and looked away. Then he seemed to have second thoughts and looking hard and questioningly he smiled again, and leaning over towards Joseph he rested his elbow on the arm of the wheelchair and whispered, 'Hi. I'm Paul Browne. Are none of your set in this class?' Joseph shook his head. 'Don't worry about being on your own,' said the new classmate. 'I'll be beside you and I'll look after you.' Joseph nearly exploded with delight. Jim Casey was standing there teaching about assonance, while under his nose real live drama was damn well in the making. Seeing but a whispering duo the teacher made no comment, after all how could he have imagined the significance of the scenario. Right there in front of him sat an able-bodied, voice-gifted youth volunteering to be a friend to a mute crippled boy.

Paul straightened up and began to turn his attention to what the teacher was saying, while Joseph sat viewing the sky outside the high window. Gulls swept back and forward in the framed picture, but he now joined them and scrambling on golden wings he mentally yelled in competition with the scavengers. I've cracked it, he yelled, I've bloodywell cracked it. Then swinging his mind back to reality, he realized that the class was nearly over and his ear had not trapped one word of Jim Casey's assonance. But anointing hope was flowing over the young student. He was amazed by Paul's boldness of approach, but time was going to prove that not only could Paul converse with his new friend but mute crippled Joseph could TALK back.

As school life daily herded him in flock formation, he silently framed questions that he wanted to put to his classmates. He pondered on the entreaties he'd like to make. His questions would test their shrewdness. He listed them: will you accept that boy's blood courses in my veins, that boy's thoughts cram my skull, boy's ambitions crowd my mind, that normal consciousness beats alongside yours? Then as though helping them he hinted: but unlike all of you, I am celibated by dank felons of armour-harnessing. He mentally moded the questions, but to his amazement his valiant friends began to frame those selfsame questions and even more wonderfully they now boldly made their observations known to him and to each other. 'Jaysus Joseph you must be damnwell driven mad by your spasms,' they said. 'Do you

wish you were just like us? ... Do you get awful fed up listening
to kids smart-arsing about you and the eejit you are with your
arms movin'? ... Do you ever wish you could give them a boot
in the arse and say "fuck off ya bleedin' prig"?' How Joseph
would react to their observations would lead them to make wider
observations about girls, sex, bastardization of all sorts, about
adults and their old-fashioned hang-ups. Joseph revelled in their
coarseness – they voiced his bloody frustrations, they gave comfort
by seeking to get inside his frame and their cursing his condition
brought laughter bubbling to his now. Sassy rasps of schoolboy's
humour cast comfort mantle-like around Joseph and friendship
cabled a denim lifeline between him and his mates.

But life was also being good to him in London: his editor was
reading and re-reading his writings. She was used to dealing with
Weidenfeld's free-voiced authors, but now she read words which
had been lifted from the depths of numbness. As she divined Boy
Joseph's plagued thoughts she became startled by the surrealism
of a creativity which had, chaos-like, nearly clung forever to the
lip of the abyss of hell.

Bragging to Paul Browne, the mute boy told him about his
coming book, about his brilliant editor, and he promised to give
him a copy some day soon.

Daffodils danced in merriment in the grounds of his school as
his mother drove in along the avenue. It was lunch hour and he
was waiting to see her car bumping over the ramp prior to coming
down the hill into the yard. She had a letter for her son, he could
see it sticking up beside the flask in her bag. But she chatted with
Paul for a while and then gripping hold of the wheelchair, she
brought Joseph inside for his lunch. Smiling and nodding he asked
what was the letter about, and mischievously she said, 'Oh! wait
till you see what it is, you'll fairly be fit to burst.' He noticed that
the envelope was large and when he saw his mother withdrawing
a catalogue he jumped with delight. The catalogue had a daffodil-
yellow cover and red letters spelled out 'New Titles Spring 1981'.
He was very excited by the words, but there inside on page
twenty-three he saw the Snowdon-taken photograph of himself.
His book's title *Dam-Burst of Dreams* was printed in large letters

and the blurb told his book's story in a nutshell.

Seeing his book's title was something special, but seeing his own name as author was truly intoxicating. His name was printed in great large script and casting his gaze over it he felt dignified, for young though he was he had already become familiar with the deceptions of life. Now here he sat among the greats of literature. He marvelled at how cradled he felt. He crowed with satisfaction, for now this book made sense of his life. Now he saw a reason for his being given a second chance at birth.

All budding writers need grand publicity, but Joseph Meehan had no voice, so schemes had to be devised by which his story and his book might be highlighted. Radio and television came to his aid and together with newspapers and magazines they stepped into his void and provided a voice for his mercurial, soundfilled words. Britain and Ireland combined in framing Joseph as a bold promising writer. BBC television joined forces with Ireland's Radio Telefis Eireann to film a documentary about him. The film crew followed the boy from bed to school, from school to his writing, from writing to his family living and family outings. Joseph filled in his thoughts into the film by having his poetry and prose doing the talking for him.

In school the film crew interviewed the headmaster, while out in the cloakroom Joseph's pals talked and planned where they'd sit for their outside interview. They combed their hair and titivated themselves. Then they got to work on their mate. They washed his face and combed his hair. Then they were ready. Trooping out of the cloakroom Paul wondered was Joseph happy with his appearance, so lifting up the wheelchair with his pal still in it, Paul held him right up in front of the high mirror. Joseph got a fleeting glimpse of a well-scrubbed face and tidy fringe and looking at Paul he gave his eyes-up signal. Walking along the corridor then Peter, Paul and Frank wondered how to handle the interview and together they tried to deduce what Joseph would think of their replies. He shook his head and laughed, indicating that he didn't give a damn. They grasped his meaning and then all laughed together. They felt clannish and really wanted to be seen to show how close they were to their friend. Sitting on the steps outside Mr Medlycott's office, Joseph's pals demonstrated how well they knew their mate and how very much like themselves he really was.

Filming outside was pleasant and cool, but then the cameras moved back inside to film a class in progress. Aileen Craig's room was the setting and her subject that morning was geography. She carried on as though the cameras didn't exist, but her pupils became all the while more rosy-cheeked from the terrible heat of the lighting.

Publicity began to build up around disabled boy-writer Joseph Meehan. Radio teams called to record documentaries about him. Magazines and newspapers sent their feature writers and photographers to visit with and interview the boy. Joseph's family showed them how their son communicated. The journalists learned his signals and learnt how communication hurried from his eyes. The ploying efforts of the boy were not wasted, for those journalists had now read the early copies of his book and no longer did they believe that handicap of the body must mean handicap of the mind as well.

Seldom a day passed that by air or sea a journalist was not wending a path to meet Joseph Meehan the author. Media folk came from all over Britain and Ireland, from Australia and Italy, from Germany and Denmark. Foolish boy that he was, he had earlier on feared for his story at the hands of sensational journalists, but now having met them he respected their professionalism. He now realized that they were straightforward people who had a job to do and a deadline to meet.

He read their articles and features, he listened to radio documentaries and watched TV documentaries. His story and writings were fairly handled. Joseph was satisfied that all journalists were the same, but the fourteen-year-old boy had a lesson coming to him.

Tall beyond the ordinary, the newcomer had to stoop down to enter through the door of the lounge. His beard was positively wild. He carried a small purple handbag and it was almost nightfall.

Slowness to grasp positive statements marked the man as

different from all the other journalists. He seemed to be missing the point. Accounts never seemed to get written down. He had trouble deciding which member of the family he should turn his guns upon. In short he worried the watching, waiting boy.

Joseph grew uneasy as questions see-sawed from the American. Giant-sized feet he seemed to put into the heart of the ear-sharp boy. Smiling never, he talked of past generations. He was obviously looking for genius, but fixed on anyone and everyone but Joseph. The crippled boy sat and sized up the questioner. He saw his naked dislike for the fools of fate. He detected an inborn aggression in the journalist and he was filled with foreboding.

Matthew detected nothing as he innocently guided the American through his family history. 'My father wrote poetry and prose and had his writings published,' he said, 'and I had a priest-uncle who was also a poet,' he added. But the tall man was not interested, Joseph could see that very clearly. Now the boy examined the route the American was taking and secretly he decided that he must show this man how he typed, and how his creative thoughts took shape. Inviting the journalist to join him, the boy typed a poem for him, but as he laboured over his work he couldn't help hearing a bored yawn. His cradled poem he gave to the American, but how was he to know that beauty was born to blush unseen.

School had to take second place to publicity, so Joseph had to miss days from class. Glancing over his glasses the headmaster said he understood, but looking sternly ponderous he warned his pupil, 'When interviews are over you must get back to school.'

School was no burden now to the disabled boy. Subjects interested him, but social experiences interested him more. His circle of buddies grew wider and his girlfriends grew haughtier. Conversation became natural and human contact got bold and beautiful.

Roll call and assembly took on a fire-and-brimstone air each Monday morning at nine o'clock sharp. Frenzied boys and girls jumped from cars and buses in a last-minute dash for school. But poor Joseph could be so near and yet so far. Stuck in his dad's car in the morning rush-hour traffic he'd sit sweating from tension.

He might be but a few trembling feet from the school gate, yet he could do nothing until the traffic moved. Then when the bleeps sounded for the nine o'clock news on the car radio he sighed and gave in. Ballyragging their students about timekeeping and study, the headmaster and class tutor would be in full flow by the time Hell's Angel himself arrived. His mates would stand there looking stonyfaced but delighting at the diversion caused by their pal's late entry. Rescuing the situation, Mr Medlycott might turn and stare over his spectacles, giving as it were the silent treatment to the lad slinking in.

Nora and Matthew worked as a team chauffering Joseph to and from school. On Wednesday 6 May it was Nora who called to bring him home for his half-day. She seated him in the front passenger seat while she stowed his wheelchair in the back of the green estate car. Chatting bubbling conversation, he didn't notice anything different about her. Reaching home, she lifted him from the car and settled him back in his wheelchair. Passing through the hall he looked at the table, but there were no letters for him. His mother wheeled him into the kitchen and gave him a glass of milk to drink. Lifting him from the chair once again, she carried him to the toilet. It was not till she had him back and seated in his chair that he noticed her opening a press, and from it she took a large padded envelope. Her face was serious as she delved inside it. He saw but a glimpse of a blue cover. Immediately he froze. His mouth fell open in astonishment. He saw now the whole book held in the hand of his smiling mother. She showed him the cover front and back. He looked at his name as it looked back at him, but he was still numb with delight. He glanced to see how his words looked in print, how his poems sat upon the page, how his prose blustered through the volume. As he looked now he saw cosy conversation bubbling out from between the anvilled sounds of his letter-talk. His mother then slowly unfolded the fingers of his clenched left hand and placed his book in his grasp. His eyes lingered upon his handful, he looked lonesomely for decisive grip, his eyes filmed with misty tears and he was overwhelmed with demented joy. He jibbed at the bit so very often but now he not only saw the answer, he held it in his own grasp.

His fingers secretly licked the hard shiny cover, he mentally calculated the yield, but his gripping fingers hesitated a moment and then splayed open, dropping his lovely golden harvest on the kitchen floor.

Fr Flynn came with communion every Wednesday and every Sunday. The day of the book was no different. The sensitive man noticed that Joseph hesitated a very long time before managing to receive the Sacred Host. Fr Flynn was never in a hurry to leave the Meehan home. He always waited for tea and a chat or an exchange of yarns. As usual he walked into the kitchen and left the boy to his thanksgiving.

Joseph's thanksgiving was fruitful. He heaved hearty tasselled thanks to his Master. He begged forgiveness for his remembering not and he bashfully necked a nod towards his book in the kitchen press. Can I brag now, he begged. Can you ever free me just long enough to vest myself for future chastening.

The quietness of Joseph's thanksgiving was halted when he peddled furiously on the steps of his wheelchair. His mother entered and casually wheeled him back into the kitchen to join her and the priest. There was a great glint in the boy's eye as he smiled at Fr Flynn. 'What's up with you, Joseph?' asked the priest, 'Did you get into trouble at school or are you up to something?' Nora opened the press and handing the envelope to Fr Flynn she said, 'He warned me not to show that till he was here to see your reaction.' 'What is it?' said the priest, and looking into the mouth of the envelope he whispered, 'It's his book, it's his book.' Drawing it out he sized it up and down and examined it inside and out. 'Joseph,' he murmured, 'congratulations, you're a marvellous fellow, it's beautiful, just beautiful.' The great and holy man was like an uncle to Joseph and Yvonne. He sat reading snippets here and there among the pages. Occasionally he smiled at the boy, hinting as it were that he joined with him in celebration of his great victory despite the terrible odds.

Thursday morning saw *Dam-Burst of Dreams* and its author off to school together. The book sat in along beside him in his chair. Fashioning himself as normal had been his schoolboy's goal and now here beside him he had his foolproof account of his desperate disabled life. Pretty well all of his class accepted that he had normal intelligence, but of course there were the doubting Thomases and book or no book, they never deviated from their pitying assessment of him. He never hoped to alter their thinking. His book was not for them; it rested beside him and he intended showing it to his friends and to his sensitive teachers.

The teachers rescued him by treating him in the same way as all of the other pupils. They checked him for messing with his pals and courageously they ignored his disability and ordered him around with the rest of the rabble. Looking at the whole staff though, Joseph found one teacher wanting. He noticed that the teacher never spoke directly to him, never asked a question to which he could give a yes or no answer – in fact he never recognized as normal the chap who was strapped into the wheelchair. Joseph's efforts went towards getting through to this man, and so he sat and eddied schemes. He bowed and bowed when the teacher asked his class if they understood his explanation of a certain concept, but how could he succeed when the teacher positively avoided looking in his direction. Joseph consoled himself by reminding himself that a staff can voice collective belief in a student, but a man convinced against his better judgment is never convinced at all.

And so he showed off his book. His friends brought him from teacher to teacher and Joseph sheepishly bowed in acknowledgement of their congratulations. Eventually his book was seized and it finished up in the staffroom. He didn't care, after all he had creamed off his credits, so why not now share his writings with his friends.

CHAPTER TWELVE

SLAVERY WAS ABOLISHED

LAUNCHING day was in June, in London, yes, in the city he had come to regard as his literary saviour. His mother was going to be his amanuensis and she had to fashion herself to be his risen voice. Radio and television producers arranged interviews with her and, coping without silent Joseph, the astute media highlighted his boy's genius, and his disability for once played second fiddle to his art. Seated in front of cameras, Nora flitted across the television screen. Her topic of conversation was her son's book. On radio too her voice nulled his handicap and chased his boy's achievements for listening ears. Joseph sat at home listening to his mother's voice funnelling his life through her eyes. Television too gave him the visual image of those responsible for framing the young author's story. But there were truly wonderful happenings in progress in London. Historically, noted names in literature were first cast in gold in London's famous Institute of Contemporary Arts, but when *Dam-Burst of Dreams* made its entry there a new corner was allotted to its young author. Emanating from Ireland and in the grand style of Beckett and Joyce, truly Irish, truly gifted, and truly bedamned, young Joseph Meehan found himself and his book hailed at the ICA Lunchtime Literary Event on 11 June 1981.

Away down south in the land of cotton, American slaves asked to have their slavery abolished. Now in downtown London in the year 1981 slavery was abolished and the free boy Joseph Meehan came forth green-grassed and blowing like an Irish Ceannbhán.

Once the book had been assessed by the great critics in the literary strongholds of England and Ireland, scholars of classics as ancient as the *Iliad* became interested in boy's boldness – bumpkin-fashioned, but vested with cloyish cleverness. As *Dam-Burst of Dreams* came on general release, Joseph found hope budding when after only ten days on the market it jumped onto the best-seller list. Fruitful machinery had released the casked clown – now Joseph's silent dreams were silent no longer.

Listowel Writer's Week was a great event in the Irish arts calendar. Running each summer, it drew writers and artists from all around the world. Truly happy but boyishly nervous, Joseph Meehan accepted his invitation to be present at the official opening as the guest of honour of the committee of Writer's Week. Never more happy and now fully relaxed, he met the organizers. Their guest speaker was Dr Brendan Kennelly, Professor of English at famed Trinity College, and on being introduced to Joseph he presented the young boy with a single fullblown rose. Until then unknown, Joseph now found himself being introduced to the vast audience. On his lap he still nursed the dark red, velvet-petalled rose with its tears of dew still nestling in their cupped fragrance. 'Nobody can make a poet,' explained Brendan Kennelly as he sought to introduce Joseph to the vast audience. 'And poety is found in the most unlikely of people,' he explained, 'but when we look at that fella in the wheelchair there, we are looking at a poet, a pure poet, he's a poet now.' Poor Joseph could barely hold back his tears and concentrated instead on the sureness of the rose's fragrance.

Clucking with fun, the great opening night turned from the young guest and pronounced itself ready for fun and festivities. He would have loved to partake of the abundant food and drink, but instead he relished in being entertained by the great artists who had gathered in circles to school him in his art. The highlight of the fun came for Joseph when John B. Keane, the playright and storyteller, decided he had advice that needed to be given to this young Meehan fellow. Bending down he whispered in Joseph's ear, 'Come over here, there's something you should know about women. You're not equipped to be a writer,' he advised,

'until you hear what I've to tell you.' And grasping hold of
Joseph's wheelchair he wheeled him over to the corner away from
listening ears on non-writers. Taking from his pocket then a great
tablecloth of a handkerchief, he first of all wiped his own mouth
and then he wiped Joseph's mouth with it as well. All was now
ready for his hushed advice, but when Joseph heard the ins and
outs of being a success with women he was grateful for his
initiation in Mount Temple boys' findings. As John B. talked,
laughter loosed from Joseph's frame while gurgles of glee gunfired
from his soul. Night became day and day never dimmed as this
grand-hearted wit and seanchai unfolded stories which man as yet
knows nothing of. People wondered what the unlikely pair had
in common but as the chat developed, John B. fell from his
comic's stool and talked of his own muse and of his own source
of inspiration, a gurgling river near Listowel. Joseph could only
nod and listen, yet he was enchanted by the conversation as it
flowed from this royal Kerryman.

Breathing success in Listowel, walking towards his future, song-
filled by the ballads of Kerry, the young boy assumed that he had
no real enemies. He strolled the streets of Listowel next morning,
he strolled them for happy hours. It was market day and he was
there to sell himself as a craftsman of words, but his countrymen
were there to sell their livestock and produce. Joseph, being the
farmer he was, revelled in the atmosphere. He sat and witnessed
hand-slapping bargaining among serious-faced horse dealers and
wily cattle jobbers. He sized up lorryloads of calves and pens of
pigs. Sun blazed down on the tar-coated streets. Quiet-standing
horses suddenly urinated musty urine; it splashed off the ground
sending droplets flying in all directions, then in artistic fashion it
scribbled away, breaking here and there into little rivulets all
chasing after their pitiful bend. Looking on, Joseph noticed the
quality of Kerry lineage. Great healthy farmers drank huge pints
of Guinness, while at the back of their minds they wondered
about the young Boyblue who had come to town to blow his
horn. Feelings of kinship nested in their glances, but how could
they have known that young Boyblue was a farmer like them.

CHAPTER THIRTEEN

THE COOL GREEN GARDEN

SERENE news greeted Joseph on his arrival home to Clontarf. His dad showed him the newspaper coverage of his Writer's Week visit to Kerry. Then abruptly changing the subject he said, 'Oh, I nearly forgot, there's a letter for you. I left it inside in the lounge.' Bringing it into the kitchen he opened it and pulled a magazine from the brown envelope. He leafed through the contents saying, 'It's the American fellow's feature.' He found the article and began reading it. He continued to read for a few minutes and then stopping abruptly he looked at Joseph. 'What is it Dad?' asked Yvonne. 'Oh, it's just a scurrilous bit of trash,' replied Matthew. Nora was preparing a meal and she turned and looked enquiringly at the magazine. Yvonne was by now reading it across her father's shoulder. Joseph was growing impatient, he peddled with his feet but Yvonne was asking, 'Can I have it, Dad, and I'll read it out loud for everyone?' She glanced at her brother and then she moved over beside him and held his pallid hand. 'Are you ready for a shock?' she warned, and squeezing his hand she began to read the article. Joseph didn't bother to look at the magazine, he just dropped his chin on his chest and listened. Yvonne sallied forward with the written assault on her brother. He listened to the journeyman's doubts, he felt the knife go in between his shoulderblades, he heard the tramp of the jackboots and scholar-like he dwelt on the origin of the writer's name. He smelt burning flesh but his body was ice-cold. 'How could he tell such lies?' pondered Nora out loud. 'How could he do that to a helpless boy?' asked Matthew. 'He shouldn't be let away with it,' grumbled Yvonne, but silent Joseph was wondering why the American chose not to mention the poem which he had purposely written in his presence.

Silence reigned when Yvonne threw down the magazine on the floor. She put her arm around her brother's shoulders and hugged him. He didn't bother to react to her concern.

Joseph Meehan the fraud, hinted the cruel big American. Joseph Meehan has a ghost writer, heralded the blundering journeyman. Joseph Meehan never allows folk to see him typing, suggested the cruel-hearted destroyer. Boy that he was, crippled though he was, naïve though he was, yet he was old enough in years and wise enough in his soul to know that evil was afoot and determinedly he resolved that he was not going to stumble.

But evil has a way of undermining the bravest. Nora saw her son struggling. She noticed that he seemed weak. She opened wide the back door into the cool green garden. The fresh air blew long lively gusts into his numb mind. Struggling but undefeated, he fought the feelings of rebellion which had now begun to burrow through his soul. Better dead, hinted his rebellious mind, but his mother seemed to sense the screeching in his silence. 'Don't heed him, Joseph,' advised Nora, 'don't heed a coward, he hasn't your guts, don't let him destroy you. Just grit your teeth and see the failure of his article.' Then placing her hand under his chin she looked into his hurt eyes and said, 'It's too early in your life to have had to confront someone like him.'

Matthew was silent for a very long time, then he festered hope in his son by saying, 'Listen Joseph, when there's not a word about him people will still be talking about you. So cheer up, don't mind him at all.'

The family jollied Joseph along, but when he went to bed that night he cried tears of pristine despair. He sobbed in silence. He was hurt. The hurt of the written assault he might forget, but the fact that a sane man had compared his frantic efforts to speak with the cry of a chastised dog left him hurt beyond freedom, beyond human hope. He blamed God. How could great God stand by and watch a dumb cripple being attacked at his very vulnerable voice?

He was now going to let God know what he thought of him. Matthew was full of chat as they strolled down Vernon Avenue that day. Joseph wasn't listening. Never once did he look back into his dad's face, never once did he smile, never once did he attempt to talk to him. Matthew didn't seem to notice, or if he did he chose to ignore it, for he was just being his usual chatty self.

Reaching the Chapel Lane entrance Matthew was wheeling him by, but Joseph suddenly jerked back and swung his head towards the church of St John the Baptist. 'Oh, do you want to drop in for a minute?' enquired his dad, as he turned the wheels and headed in along the lane.

Wheels swished on the aisle as Matthew wheeled Joseph up towards the altar. Genuflecting in front of the hidden Christ, his dad got into a seat and knelt down to say a prayer. His son sat idly gazing about. He ignored the tabernacle.

Matthew finished his prayer and looking at Joseph he whispered, 'Are you ready?' Joseph nodded. His dad genuflected again and turning the wheelchair, he set off down the aisle. But his son jumped and nodded towards the side chapel. 'What,' said Matthew, 'do you want to see the crucifix?' He wheeled him over and there hanging up on the wall was a lifesize Christ crucified to a huge black cross. His pallid limp body sagged windswept and dead. Crowned with thorns, his grey face was streaked by caked blood, his wonderful eyes were turned vacantly upwards, his head fell backwards and his veins were taut in his throat. Feet and hands held him crested to the cross. But Joseph was not seeing the sadness of the spectacle that day, his boy's heart was broken and he knew who to blame. The bright angry eyes of the rebellious boy looked up at the great crucifix and swinging his left arm in a grand arc he made the two-finger sign at the dead Christ. Breathing noisily he looked at his dad and with a brazen sweep of his head he ordered him to wheel his chair away.

Hell held no greater devil that day. Joseph Meehan had been tested and yielded. He felt powerful though, he tasted new frantic joy. He told God what he thought of him and his cross. He was furious still.

Matthew wheeled him along. He bought the evening paper in Furlongs, but Joseph didn't seem to notice. The untimely paper held no place in his battle. The boy held his head down. He was deep in thought. But Hell has its own torments. He was only half-way up the avenue on his way home when Hell began its loud laughing. Imagine telling God to fuck off, thus the niggling began. Imagine saying fuck off to the crucified Christ. Imagine having the nerve to be obscene in front of the crucifixion.

Matthew noticed nothing different about his disabled boy. He drew Joseph's attention to a football match in St Anne's Park. 'Will we go in and have a look?' asked his dad, but Joseph shook his head very deliberately. Christ had now bespoked sadness and the boy hesitated; the sadness struck again but the heart hesitated. A bird twittered suddenly. Sadness stole stealthily into his soul. A car horn beeped and Joseph lifted his head just in time to see the wicked grin of his now great friend John Flynn. Then like a bolt of lightning his soul jumped. He'll be bringing me communion the day after tomorrow, scolded his conscience, now what am I going to do, he hassled.

Sealed within his bony prison he lay in bed that night. He detected his gilded cage bars, but caged birds sing sweetly, taunted his despair. Vanity, vanity, all is vanity, hinted his sanity, but with the thought came comfort duck-down-softly stealing to bed his boy's cold voice.

He who eats and drinks unworthily eats and drinks judgment for himself, reminded his conscience. Joseph worried himself with the thought. Vanity had been his sin, despair made him fall.

Saturday was always a busy day in the Meehan stockade. Breathing normality into their situation, they fretted and ferreted for fun, as though numbness cradled credit. Nora shopped and baked, cooked and cleaned, sometimes roping in her daughter to help her. Fresh flowers rested in vases, honesty breasted her motives. She cringed from fresh hurt when she saw the handiwork of the American, but hers was a crested gold heart and forgiveness came thick and fast for the man and his motives.

Fretting for his soul's state, Joseph too needed forgiveness. Since nobody knew of his rebellion, nobody could help. There he sat in the kitchen, watching his family make ready for Sunday while he couldn't make ready at all. Nora was storing away the shopping, and as she stacked onions in a plastic container she detected that her store of potatoes was low. Turning to the family she said, 'Do you know what I forgot to get – potatoes – now who'll volunteer to go for some?' Yvonne continued reading the newspaper. She believed in keeping her head down until trouble was past. So Joseph made his move and giving a jump in his seat, he nodded towards Matthew. 'Don't be looking at me,' said his dad, 'I won't be here tomorrow so I'll not be needing spuds.' Nora laughed and looking at Joseph she said, 'He'll give in. Just keep working on him.' Joseph was in need of confession, and how to get to the church was his stumbling block, so he began his nodding, begging game, continuing it until his dad said, 'How do you intend carrying the bag of potatoes?' Joseph hinted that he'd carry them on his lap. 'Alright,' said Matthew, 'here we go and we'll just bring a plastic bag of them.' He fetched Joseph's anorak and hustled him into it, then off they wheeled towards the shop.

So far so good thought the boy, as his dad pushed him along through the supermarket. Talking comradely, they had decided on a half-stone bag of Golden Wonders. Matthew placed them on his son's lap and turned for home. But Joseph looked back enquiringly into his eyes. 'What do you want?' he asked the boy. 'Do you want to go somewhere else?' Joseph flicked his eyes upwards. 'Well tell me where,' said Matthew, 'look up when I come to the right place.' His father named all of the likely venues but Joseph made no stir, and then as an afterthought he said, 'Maybe it's the church?' Joseph tossed his eyes upwards. 'Ah do we have to traipse all that way down there?' said weary Matthew, but his son put on a sad begging demeanour and the fond heart of the father crested manly forgiveness and turned down the road to the church on the seafront.

I'll be rightly fecked if he's not here after all my scheming, berated the boy silently. If his car is here he'll be somewhere about. But on their way in through the heavy doors of the church they walked slap-bang into the priest himself. 'What are you doing with the spuds, Meehan?' teased the hearty man. Joseph laughed but his eyes were pleading. He spotted the purple stole rolled up in Fr Flynn's hand. He glanced into the priest's eyes and carried his gaze downwards towards his hand. It failed to give his hint. He tried again. Matthew was blatterin' something about Leitrim, while under his nose his son was trying to work a miracle. Fr Flynn had now looked away and he too was blathering about his Leitrim. Joseph paced himself, he watched the face of the priest and waited to make his next move. Now the holy man was looking at him and he started his eye game again. 'We'll push on,' said Matthew, but Joseph was trying to gimlet his eyes into Fr Flynn's face. 'Wait,' said the priest, 'do you want to tell me something?' Now Matthew got interested and he came around to face his son. Joseph continued to bow at the priest's hand and to look back again at his face. 'It's my hand he's looking at,' said Fr Flynn opening his grasp, and there his stole lay before him. 'Do you want to make your confession, Joseph?' asked John Flynn and Joseph Meehan leapt in his chair.

The wheels hugged the aisle as woman hugs her firstborn. Umpteen times had his chair swished up the church, but now heavyladen with sins including savage-signalled obscenity and a half-stone bag of Golden Wonders, it laboured under its heavy load. Fr Flynn pushed the wheelchair along and turning across to the side chapel and settling the brakes into locking position, he left the boy sitting beneath the feet of the hanging dead Christ. Placing his stole around his neck the priest stood in for Christ and on resurrecting his penitent's soul from the knacker's yard, he absolved Joseph in the name of the Blessed Trinity.

Joseph Meehan, the sinner that was, dallied in fields of delight as he chortled his way home that Saturday. He glanced back into his father's face and smiled in happy glee. 'You're in great form,' commented Matthew, 'you must have been in a bad way to have your kettle scraped,' he said. His son laughed outright and glanced his affirmative signal many and many a time.

Nourished by his communion next morning and sensing untold happiness, Joseph masked himself behind the figure of his backer. Mouthing thankfulness he pleaded for his bygones and his hasbeens. Seeing bliss greeting his talk-styled thoughts, he crowed to join in with his family and the priest in their hilarity and conversation. His mother entered and wheeled him into the kitchen. She told John Flynn of the American's assault on Joseph, she told him how upset her son was at being dubbed a fraud. The priest listened carefully and then looking at the young boy he said, 'Ah Joseph, don't be such an eejit. Yer man wanted to create a controversy. Just realize that the American people aren't fools, they'll be able to read between the lines.'

But books, journalists, photographers and even great-hearted Fr Flynn were going to be left behind in Dublin. The family needed rest and freedom to be themselves. Trembling from the assault on his honesty, the boy now joined with them as they packed their bags for their two weeks' break in Kerry. They needed to relax and Joseph needed time to lick his wounds and build his resolve to go on writing and go on being true to himself.

The holiday had to be all things to all members of the Meehan family. To Matthew it meant golf, to Nora it meant rest and a break from cooking and cleaning, to Yvonne it meant freedom from study, time for socializing and games of tennis, while to Joseph it meant long happy hours fishing by the lapping river with fresh company bestowed by thoughts of the Celtic monks of the Great Skellig Rock.

Skellig Rock yielded a secret line of longitude to the typhooned boy's desert. Ever since he first noticed its distant spires he felt captivated. He first glimpsed its craggy, spired finger and thumb one late sunset scan when looking out to sea. It beckoned to him to come out and taste its isolation. Beautifully silhouetted, it stamped its image upon his mind. Fashioned by nature, washed by vast ocean currents, Skellig Michael created vociferous vibes in his anointed heart.

The Great Skellig was born out of the sea. Twelve miles of water cut it off from the mainland of Ireland. Though uninhabited now, it stood there as a monument to early man's power over the elements of nature and despair. Crested upon its face long centuries ago clung a small band of anchorite monks, early Christians, creating a heaven out of nature's hell. Building their beehive huts from crude stone, they sheltered from the roaring winds; sucked to doleful rock, they heard messaged grace flow into their hearts. Not having enough clay with which to bury their dead, they navigated mountainous seas in search of land, and bringing back the soil in canvas-covered boats, they carried it up the six hundred roughly hewn steps to their artificial graveyard.

> Scorched by burning summer sun
> And burnt by frosty red moon
> They suffered night and noon:
> But when daylight lit their
> Morning sky, dawn welcomed forth
> A band on high to see their
> Victory blaze the sky.

Joseph told himself this story each time sadness plagued him or cloyed rancour budded young rebellion. Mugged by normal, able-bodied man, he came now to Kerry to join anew with cosy, Skellig-beasted man. Crippled though he was, he climbed the mental, stony stairway to build fashioned, lovely boyhood astride Skellig's sane name, and in the company of birds he sampled casted Christ yelling out of beehive huts, while nutshelled meaning glanced dictionary-grasp to the clown-faced puffin's cry.

The family were all rested, tanned and ready for action when they returned from their holiday in the Kingdom County. Humdrum life waited for Joseph, but now he was in charge again. He forgave the American journalist and viewed his feature from a different perspective.

CHAPTER FOURTEEN

'head the ball'

LOVELY summer edged away and Boyblue had now to bygone the days of fun and bud new courage for the year ahead. Mount Temple re-opened in September and now Joseph faced fifth year and fresh challenge. Again he found himself stranded. As was necessary his friends had to change subjects, and therefore had to move up or back the word Dublin. Joseph's subjects remained the same while theirs had to cater for their strengths or weaknesses. Bending towards his needs, he now found new boys and girls seeking to befriend him. Stephen Monahan, Greg Gallagher, Helen Sheil, Dawn Glover and John Keely took him on, and figuring out his method of communication they created joy and comradeship where solitude could have named him lonely. Teachers never molly-coddled him; he was on his own and he either created his own friends or fell by the wayside. Fortunately for him though, boys and girls in fifth year cast care around him and together with all of his old friends made new blossoms grow on his lone-bushed life.

Seated alongside his new friends he golloped up new byways of fun and new bygones of class. Excuses became rich and highly imaginative when pals wished to avoid French, art, history or maths. Looking in through a peephole in the classroom door they studied form. 'Have we been missed?' they wondered, 'Can we chance going in late?' they mused, as stealthily they turned down the door handle, but on finding the door locked, they rejoiced and set off down the corridor in search of freedom. Excuses were made if they met the class tutor. Calling them to task, the desperate tutor sometimes believed their story that they were either going on or coming from doing an errand for their class teacher. Joseph enjoyed perfect health, but he had oftentimes to feign illness in order to back up their excuse for wishing to bring him outside for air. But whatever the ploy, once outside they held, as John Keely described them always, 'woeful philosophical conversations'.

Joseph cunningly nailed his friends cruelly hard in school, but at home he nailed his family in similar vein. His book brought notoriety to him as well as his family. They hurrahed his husked history, but by being close to him they too found themselves in the limelight. Nodding his head around his all-youthful scene, he secretly chortled at the struggles of his family. His mother feared for her son, while he cast amused glances in her direction. She was invited to London to Britain's Women Of The Year Luncheon at the Savoy Hotel. She was to be their guest of honour. The theme of the luncheon speeches was the question 'Who Cares?' It was the International Year of Disabled People and Nora was invited to be a speaker on the day.

Joseph sat watching his mother as she drafted her speech. Tossing one attempt after another into the wastepaper basket, she used the excuse 'I can only speak for four minutes' as her reason for scrapping so many drafts. Then seeing her son sniggering, she rounded on him, 'So well you can laugh, look what you walk me into. I've never spoken to more than three or four people at any one time, and now because of you I've to address the cream of Britain's women, and all six or seven hundred of them at that. So wipe that grin off your face if you know what's good for you.'

'Don't worry Mam,' said Yvonne, 'I'll hold the fort while you're away.' Nora was spending a long weekend in London. Matthew fed Joseph and carried him to bed and to the toilet. Yvonne did the housework, the shopping and the cooking. Adapting herself well she asked Matthew, 'Did Joseph's bowels work?' 'No,' said Matthew, 'but don't worry, he'll be more relaxed when his Mam comes home.' Joseph agreed wholeheartedly with his dad, but Yvonne was running the show and that included Joseph's bowels. So, despite a big showdown, he had to give in to his sister but secretly he knew he didn't need any Milk of Magnesia – and most certainly he didn't need two desertspoonfuls of it – but that's precisely what he got. Yvonne was proud of her nursing skills and Joseph was equally proud of his stamina. Quietly he waited for his bowels to work, and just as quietly they decided not to.

Credit stamped Nora's speech at the Savoy Luncheon. The function took place in the presence of HRH Princess Anne. BBC radio broadcast a programme covering the highlights of the famous event. Joseph sat in Clontarf listening to his mother's voice coming from London, and to his boyish delight he too smiled accordingly as she took a standing ovation from Britain's Women Of The Year.

But now she was back in Dublin and it was business as usual. She drove her son to school. He thought no more of the Magnesia but his bowels remembered. The laxative just waited until his science class had started and then it began its battle to humiliate him. Boldly he decided he'd concentrate on what Mrs Leech was teaching and his guts would then rest easy, but resolutions have no effect on Magnesia. Here he was trying to outwit his bowels whilst fellas on motorbikes zoomed about his belly. They became busier, but Joseph flagged them down. They roared desperately, but he held them back. Frightened but not budging, certainly worried but still gnashing his teeth, he felt hot then cold. Sweat, cold and moist, clammed his face, clouds black as night blurred his vision, blood veins cramped his legs, crisis faced him squarely, and bearing in mind that he couldn't get relief until Nora came at lunchtime, he gasped out loud. Classmates glanced a fleeting glance, but trembling success still was his. Certain brightness of vision heralded the fact that he had won this round, but what about the next? As class came to an end Joseph saved his reputation. Beaming at his friend, Avril, he feasted on the cold air in the corridor.

Class resumed after the mid-morning break and all hands listened to their science lesson. But science had no answer for hassled, dosed fellows who if not forced to take laxative would not now be in such agony of mind and bowel. Sitting beside him, Avril Henderson suddenly detected the beads of sweat clinging to his face and taking a dry tissue from the pocket of his wheelchair, she wiped his face saying under her breath, 'Are you alright, Joseph?' He nodded, what else could he do? He knew he cast roles of responsibility on his fresh-faced friends, but bringing him to the toilet was a chore he would never ask them to do for him. After all he called on them to speak for him when he found himself under duress. He relied on them to wheel him hither, thither and yon. He let them know he dearly appreciated their wiping his nose or mouth for him. He craved them to force his teeth apart when a spasm of his jaw muscles accidently caught his fleshy inside cheek or his busy foolish-merited tongue in a vice-grip which he himself could release only following a spent spasm or a sudden frightened reflex movement. They, those wonderful girls and boys, gave of themselves, polishing his every day with their loyal caring. They never made a compliment. They brought others into their circle. They ranted about those snobbish students treating Joseph as dross by ignoring his very presence among them. But Joseph saw deeper. He saw the consternation in the gaze of seemingly coldhearted students. He detected a contradiction rampant in their minds, feelings of helplessness barred their approach, meaningful curtness covered a frightened consciousness. Allowing for his friends, he now determinedly held on. I'll wait till lunchtime, he counselled himself, but the fierce griping pains spearheaded attack after attack. He felt weak, worried and hopeless. If I could get my hands on Yvonne, he thought, but before he could decide on a form of torture for her the motorbike riders were revving up for off again. Distraught, he creased his body in a last effort to save his dignity.

At the end of class the students were invited to see a travelling theatre group stage frolicsome feats of drama in the cleared library. The group of players was magnificent, but the role of clown bullied and bashed a boy until he surrendered. Now he felt humanly hurt, his was the shame, his the humiliation.

Washed of guilt, Joseph felt consoled when Nora said, 'What else could you do?' But Paul Browne was hopping mad. 'Why didn't you tell me and I'd have brought you to the toilet, or failing that I'd have phoned your mother, but no, you had to do

Superman, so bloody careful, not wantin' to be a trouble. What sort of a friend are you?' badgered his mate. But contrary to her nursing practice, poor Yvonne was shattered. Nora read the riot act to her about she daring to impose her will on her brother. But when the family were asleep that night, demented Yvonne stole across the landing and crept into his room. 'Are you asleep, Joseph?' she whispered, and seeing his head turn towards her she declared, 'Damn me and my bullying, I'm awful sorry for causing you all that suffering.' He tried to say forget it, but she placed her hand lightly over his mouth saying, 'Ssh, don't wake them. I just want to say I'm very, very sorry. I'll make up to you for what I did, you just see if I don't,' and giving his cheek a brushed kiss, she was gone as silently as she came.

Crestfallen after his ordeal with the laxative, he soon forgot his humiliation. Now life was bolstering his ego and stirrings of joy were again cradling his boy's heart. He had won distinction in Britain on three separate occasions. Now he had just been notified that in Ireland he had been nominated for a 'People Of The Year' award.

The night of the awards was one of the most spectacular nights of his life. He was only sixteen years of age, yet the judges cited him as having made 'an outstanding contribution to society in Ireland'. It was the International Year of Disabled People, so the organizers requested their youngest recipient ever to address the entire gathering. Joseph was stunned, firstly by receiving the nomination, and secondly by being chosen as one meriting an award. Now his being chosen to speak to the huge gathering of government representatives, members of the Seanad, distinguished members of the judiciary, medical experts, educational and academically qualified dignitaries and representatives of all branches of the media, left silent Joseph more silent still. Zoo-caged for so long, schottische-mimed movements his natural paraphernalia, bastioned inside the arena for fools but now broken free, he was going to grace the function by his very presence there.

Wearing a bow tie, vivacious but silent, Joseph was wheeled up through the society-bedecked tables to the huge decorated stage. An army team played a triumphant fanfare as he approached the stage. All the men and women were on their feet; the applause was breathtakingly wonderful; the cripple was flummoxed by the joisting music of hundreds of hands clapping his very existence.

As he festooned himself with glory, he sampled the aeon's awe contained within the applause of those hundreds and hundreds of people. Looking down at them from his vantage point, he watched their reaction to his address. Looking up at him tears were hurriedly wiped away but he didn't pretend to notice for he had a job to do and a destiny to accede to.

He glanced often at his mother. There she stood conveying his words for him. She it was who gambled with her sensibilities and got from his signals the gist of his thoughts. Now she stood at the podium holding his typewritten words in her hand and read: 'A brain-damaged baby cannot ponder why a mother cannot communicate with it, and unless it gains parental love and stimulation it stymies, and thus retardation fulsomely establishes its soul-destroying seabed.' Conscious of the breathtaking sacrifice involved in what his family did for him, yet he detected where destiny beckoned. The future for babies like him never looked more promising, but now society frowned upon giving spastic babies a right to life. Now they threatened to abort babies like him, to detect in advance their handicapped state, to burrow through the womb and label them for death, to baffle their mothers with fear for their coming, and yet, the spastic baby would ever be the soul which would never kill, maim, creed falsehood or hate brotherhood. Why then does society fear the crippled child, wondered Joseph out loud, and why does it hail the able-bodied child and crow over what may in time become a potential executioner?

With applause thundering in his soul, his wheelchair was lifted down from the stage, he returned to his parents. The son who dallied in the temple and talked to the scribes now sat amazing his family and cradling them in his glory.

Quietly his uncle Joe Murtagh slipped a bottle of champagne in along beside him in his wheelchair. 'You don't eat or drink in public,' he said, 'but when you get home break open this champagne and sample something of what you have given us here tonight.' Then slapping his nephew on the back and with a huge wink he said, 'Now don't drink too much or you'll be sorry tomorrow.'

People unlikely to make their feelings known came to Joseph's side, and bending down, they poured their glorious compliments into the young boy's ear. He smiled and bowed, he bowed and smiled; he was intoxicated before he even tasted his Uncle Joe's champagne.

Night-time brought possible meaning to his glittering night in the Burlington Hotel. Fretting no longer, his vision became golden bright as nimbly he looked for footprints on his hassled road to heaven.

Were the great events of last night but a beautiful dream, mused the silent boy as he surfaced from his sleep next morning, or did I really speak to all those hundreds of people as they for once just listened. Wait till I tell Fr Flynn, he bragged. He'll surely say, 'Rubbish, did the people not realize that you write rubbish?' Joseph greatly admired the humility of the man – everyone and everything held precedence over himself. He humbled Joseph often by hinting of his being but a servant while he decorated the young boy with the title 'poet'.

Usually joyful, John Flynn found honest happiness when he sat in the Meehan kitchen. Never holier-than-thou, he knew he shouldn't be smoking and he needing heart surgery, but he'd get the ashtray and setting it down beside him he'd light his cigarette, and taking a great pull he'd inhale the smoke so deep that Joseph would expect it to seep from his shoes.

But came the day when, without being noticed, he didn't make a beeline for the ashtray. Seeming nonchalant he chatted in his usual manner. Matthew was the first to notice. 'Are you off cigarettes?' he questioned. All manner of enquiring eyes turned towards Fr Flynn and he, very casual, very dismissive of his great sacrifice said, 'Ah sure I gave them up. The surgeon said "No smoking ever again, if you do I won't operate on you." Ye know that I've to have a bypass job done on my heart?' As everyone knew only too well that he wished to defer surgery for as long as possible in order to care for his nonagenarian mother, his comment came as a reminder of how charitable he was in catering for Joseph's needs as well. Then in order to change the subject he called out, 'Are you finished in there head-the-ball, come out, I've a great yarn to tell you.' With vivacious eyes twinkling with merriment he sat waiting for Joseph to be wheeled from the lounge into the kitchen, and now satisfied that feelings of fear for his condition were dismissed, he fashioned yarn after yarn, always watching for fun-filled reaction from the disabled boy. Fr Flynn's efforts moved Yvonne to try shocking him with her latest gags from college, and the hearty laughs guffawing from the priest gave the impression that he had not noticed the message which must have been nudging in his mind.

Knocking very gently, breathless with regret, Deirdre Devine knocked on the window first and then more hesitantly on the door. She feared her terrible task; she it was who had to break the mournful news to Joseph. She hesitated by enquiring, 'Did you hear the news?' and Nora suspecting punishing news said, 'No, what?', and gripping Nora's arm but keeping her troubled gaze on Joseph she said, 'It's Fr Flynn.' Frowning her forehead she fretted to find a way of fitting the boy for his crisis news. 'It's his mother?' numb Nora suggested. Nora was attempting to fend for her son but Deirdre's whimper put paid to that observation. 'All I can tell you,' she said, 'is that he failed to come out for the 7.30 Mass this morning. Seeing that the time was passing someone called to the house and he was found dying. There was just time for a priest to anoint him,' she added. Nora turned to Joseph and putting her hand on his shoulder she squeezed it tightly. Yells broke from his crippled body, forgetting that boys shouldn't cry, especially before strangers, his sobs sent gentle Deirdre home to compose herself after her acute ordeal.

What will his poor mother do to heal her cold fretting, worried the now quietened boy. But trembling God saw to her: he heaped confusion on her aged thinking so that she was never lucid long enough to piece together assorted frantic longings with rusty reality.

Fr John Flynn's Requiem Mass was at eleven o'clock in the Church of St John the Baptist and following the Mass, his funeral took place to lonely, rocky Leitrim. Years ago he had left his boyhood home to undertake his great, frank ministry and now his work wrought, his mortal white-clad bones traversed the route in reverse to be trimmed no longer by service, but by the numbing, lapping sound of Lough Allen's waters by which he nested now in heather-hued heath.

CHAPTER FIFTEEN

THE SOUND OF FOOTSTEPS

L IFE had changed, changed suddenly, and yet again Joseph was seeking out human understanding. Now he looked around for a priest who could step in to John Flynn's vacant shoes.

Perhaps my uncle will sympathize with my needs, mused the handicapped boy. Maybe he can bring the sacraments to me. Maybe he can leave his monastery just long enough to help a poor fellow in a fix.

Fr Patsy Meehan left his monastery each Sunday, and in his pocket he carried the pyx bearing the communion bread for his nephew. Borrowing prayers from the Psalms he spoke as young Joseph would:

> 'Sprinkle me oh Lord with hyssop
> and I shall be cleansed;
> Wash me, and I shall be made
> whiter than snow.'

With all of the understanding and patience of an uncle, the priest held aloft the Sacred Host, and with prayers silently moving his lips he learnt to wait until his nephew had guided his muscles through their difficulties. Sunday after Sunday his uncle called and with each visit came deeper understanding of the bothered ways of his nephew.

Communion served to join the silent boy with silent God, and into his masked ear Joseph poured his mental whispering, begging blessings to be showered on his faithful friends. He looked out on scattered continents whispering his awe and pleaded for his brothers and sisters as though skin colour was but a variation of family crests. Wisdom seemed to wise him to see his awful boyhood as though awfulness was beautiful. His heard secrets cradled him and fruit served yet again to form on hilltopped briar.

Joseph prayed too for his grandparents, for the breasted bravery which they exhibited in their life's journey through Westmeath. Living at either end of the county he remembered two of the four. Matthew's mother he remembered for her softness and humility. Living in Glenidan, she had spent herself teaching in the school that looked out upon the wonders of Fore. She always schemed to have trifle in the fridge, knowing that her grandson could readily digest the jelly-based dessert. She thought of his condition by omitting the usual sherry – after all, she didn't want to set him drunk – but he knew he was more than capable of acting that part himself.

Joseph considered it normal to have but one grandmother and one grandfather. His mother's father buttressed him in a unique way. Honesty looked out from his grandfather's gaze and the sound of his footsteps stamped themselves for all times in his boy's consciousness. Joseph spent holidays with him hubbing schemed notions of how best to cope with his handicap.

Nora's father built up his dairy herd and far-flung farms by besting his tired body to go on working despite his weariness. Rearing his family, he gapped on attention for himself. When he chatted with Joseph he overlooked his handicap and advised Nora to allow the child to experiment for himself. Rolling a ball along the floor, he left Joseph down on it and said: 'Go on now and get that ball yourself.' Joseph lifted himself up on his hands and looked after the ball, but decided it was out of reach. His grandfather rolled him over on his back and coaxed, 'Now go that way and you'll get it.' Sampling freedom, his grandson pushed with his heels, but he found he was inclined to go round in circles. The friendly grandfather played with his handicapped grandchild, but always he seemed to be searching for voluntary movements in the boy. Placing a wooden spoon in his grasp, he guided the youngster's hand and showed him how to make a noise by hinting,

'Come on, we'll beat blazes out of this cake tin,' and together the generations joined and together assembled bedlam where heretofore anointed silence reigned.

Breakfast time in Clonbonny looked great to the silent, watching boy. Work was in progress in the farmyard while in the kitchen waited the table all set ready for the hungry team to enter. Porridge steamed in readiness but when grandsons need nourishment, farmers know what to give them. Porridge for Joseph needed something special to be added. Seizing a blue-banded jug, off would step his grandfather jug in hand towards the dairy across the yard. The footsteps could be heard stamping back towards the kitchen and the boy would just look impish, when on returning his grandfather would bespoke hearty hope by saying, 'Come on now Joseph, I want to see you eating a big breakfast, I have something here that'll put hair on your chest.' And slowly pouring thick golden cream over his grandson's porridge he'd quirk an eyebrow and say, 'Get that inside you and then I'll bring you out and we'll scour for mushrooms in the horse park or fish for pinkeens.' His was the bribe and his grandson always went for the bait. Clonbonny was very much a part of his childhood scene. He slept in the room over the kitchen and while waiting for sleep to come, he could always listen to voices chatting and laughing as folk came and went about their business.

Clonbonny held a Station every springtime and every autumn. The custom dated back to the days when the savage Penal Laws forbade attendance at Mass and priests had a bounty on their heads. But they were safe with their flock and managed to celebrate the great sacrifice in isolated dwellings or on hillside rocks, while single-minded lookouts scanned surrounding countryside for fresh messengers of oppression.

Now the days of awful persecution were well past, but the custom lingered on. The Station now expressed community celebration, cementing of neighbourliness, continuity of family contact and bonding of country people's folklore and values. Time occasioned a lapse of seven years between one Station and the next in the family rota of the district, so between the two celebrations time could wield its scythe, selecting and mowing down its harvest from the host family. But seven years on, the Station would again be celebrated and new faces would light the host's smile of welcome to celebrant and congregation alike.

Joseph was now a full-blooded Molly Malone, but still he answered the beckoning to the Station in Nora's childhood home. Lights twinkled from the many windows, flowers scented the night air, voices grew in volume welcoming friend, neighbour and family members flown the nest. At eight o'clock the accounter of pardon arrived and conversation took on a low key as one penitent after another sampled forgiveness for confessed sins. 'Anyone else for confession?' was questioned from one room to the next all the way down to the kitchen and back went the answer, 'Everyone's been.' Now another enquiry made the rounds, 'Who's for communion, hands up please?' There a member of the family stood on tiptoes, fingering the count before returning to tell the priest how many wafers to place in the ciborium.

Now absolute silence reigned as the priest robed himself in vestments and Mass began with the sign of the cross. Every room was crowded, people stood in the hall and even on the steps of the stairs, but the voice of the priest encompassed his congregation and together they gave praise and thanks to God.

Joseph sat three rooms away from the communion table but the tinkle of the warning bell told him that the moment of consecration was nigh. A tinkle rang out again and he could visualize the raised host. A second bell told of an elevated chalice. Now Christ was among his people and soon he came towards each communicant under the guise of the eucharist.

Mouthing his thanks, Joseph rescued himself once again. He cradled his family in his prayers, praying grace and strength to each one of them as they struggled with their cross. He held his head bent down in thought and then a faint glow warmed his heart, for suddenly he sensed he heard the sound of footsteps walking back across the yard to the kitchen.

Prayers ended and then Mammon reigned. Nora and her sisters brought everyone together to sup and feast at their leisure. Generations garnered people together and to his delight, Joseph found himself in the kitchen among all the young fellows and girls. He sized up his cousins; they dreamed of futures in family situations like that around them, but he freed himself of any such hope just as they would free themselves of hesitance, chair-boyed and solitary. But his was a fleeting thought – fun was of the making and food was for consumption. The chat was laughter-laden, the teasing was good-natured and in time the cheer of his wine warmed the worries of the world and left but a wrinkle.

Joseph placed great store by being a member of a family. Better dead, he felt, than be sent to an institution or a hospital. He was always prepared to go anywhere for educational purposes, but he felt he would need to be brought home at weekends and holidays. Now he had the best of both worlds, he found education at Mount Temple while he could claim membership of his family at home in Clontarf.

Fifth year was an exam-free year in Mount Temple, so his pals made the most of their freedom. Faced with the schemes of fifth years, the teachers rode out the storm as best they could. 'No smoking in the school' ran the strict rule, but behind the science building could be found groups of boys smoking as though the rule didn't exist. Fifth and sixth years claimed this area as their territory and there, almost to a man, they clustered in groups, smoking and chatting. One man couldn't but wished he could, while to a man one group tried to help him. Stephen put the lit cigarette in Joseph's mouth but no use, he couldn't grip it with his numb lips. Peter decided then to hold his mouth closed on the fag and then together they all said, 'Pull, damn you Joseph, can't you pull.' He looked up at them and laughed. 'Hold it,' said Paul, 'I've a brainwave,' and putting back the now damp-ended fag in Joseph's mouth they repeated the operation, but this time Paul held Joseph's nose and now, fag in his mouth, his mouth held tightly closed and with Paul squeezing his nose, they all shouted 'PULL,' and what else could he do but pull. He was fit to burst for want of breath, so that when he pulled he pulled with every ounce of his strength. Smoke gushed down his gullet into his lungs, his stomach and his bladder, and after what seemed an age it belched back in a coughing fit surely meant to signal death. The boys stood aghast, mouths open in anticipation and as he coughed he couldn't stop, for now he was laughing not only at himself but at the terrified expressions on his experimenters' faces. Eventually he stopped choking and to a man they told him, 'Ya bleedin' well nearly choked, you'll not frighten us like that again.' Laughing still and fretting not at all, Joseph knew then that that moment and that smoke would forever filter through his blue dawns.

Life was never done consoling and surprising young Joseph Meehan. When he least expected, something else would happen to heap glory on his boyhood. People gave of themselves in their planning another great honour for the disabled boy. BBC television joined forces with Granada television authorities to fly Joseph and his family to England. It was the close of the great International Year of Disabled People and they jointly looked towards Joseph as their guest. Television producers and presenters set out to examine society's reaction to the year. They had earlier on posed questions to the crippled boy, and now in their programmes they thought fit to use his typed answers.

Rivalry between authorities was forgotten as the two stations united in their efforts to inbed joy in his life. Restfully he nodded his head in acknowledgement of their thoughtfulness. He was given an inside look and detailed instruction on every facet of television and broadcasting. His every comfort was considered. His hotel suite was booked in readiness for his need for privacy when dining, and he was very moved by the spirit which he saw in people who for the most part were used to interviewing voice-gifted, able-bodied people.

Gracing their acknowledgement of his creative ability, they booked a marvellous outing for Joseph and his family. Their secret wish was to give the boy the experience of a lifetime. Seats were booked at the Royal Shakespeare Theatre in Stratford-Upon-Avon and the play on the night was *A Midsummer Night's Dream*.

Every boy needs friends, but when Joseph Meehan arrived at the theatre he was amazed at the forethought which had gone into planning his night out. Breathing brought him worry for sometimes his could be noisy and he would be fearful of spoiling the night out for other people, but on his arrival at the theatre he was met by the manager and staff. Welcoming him as though he were a royal personage, they lifted his chair and as a team they carried him up the carpeted flights of stairs to the director's box. Joseph felt like a pope, as carried aloft in his gestatorial chair he looked down on his helpers and wondered. But when he found himself in the soundproof box getting a bird's-eye view of the breathtaking performance he puzzled, what, all this for a fair-haired Irish boy?

Loyal friends he had at home, but here he was a stranger being clasped to bosoms as though he were special. His was an acute sensitivity, but never once did he doubt the respect or the motive of those thoughtful child-bearers.

Folk magic left him spellbound, lighting was breathtakingly beautiful, sound effects came bursting into his consciousness as *A Midsummer Night's Dream* unfolded before him. 'How happy some o'er other-some can be!' best expressed his enjoyment, but at the core of his happiness nudged the thought of crippled brothers and sisters who had gone before him. He hurt for their never having had a chance to experience such cradled beauty but he could not let the thought spoil his experience, so winding down his curtain, he convinced himself that the cruelties of life have their shadows crossed by magic in the guise of gossamer-flung dreams.

The flight back to Dublin capped a wonderful event-filled trip to England. Joseph's mind was chockfull of experiences and his debt to the able-bodied man had become so great that he felt bankrupt in the face of it. Sitting in the plane his mind tossed over his dazzling boyhood's findings. He marvelled again and again at the humility within the human heart. He noticed how reticent is the person in the face of afflicted brother man, but with charity the gap becomes closed and smiles become natural. Such was his thinking when suddenly a hand rested lightly on his shoulder. 'Aren't you the boy I saw on television?' enquired the pretty hostess. 'I saw you yesterday and your poetry fascinated me.' Joseph bowed and smiled and then bending down near his ear she whispered, 'I'm honoured to have you on my flight, wait till I tell my parents that I had Joseph Meehan on my flight to Dublin.'

Lunch was now being served, and sitting beside her brother Yvonne explained that Joseph didn't dine in public. But prior to touching down at Dublin Airport the hostess came to him and there, packed in an airline bag, was a lovely lunch for the boy. 'Have that when you get home,' she said, 'and we put in some red wine and some white 'cause we felt you could always share a bottle with your sister.'

As Joseph drank his white wine that evening he felt happy beyond his dreams. He tried to distinguish whether his great happiness was as a result of his trip to Britain or his British Airlines wine drunk excessively and enjoyed too well. But then he couldn't wait to decide, for his family noticed his sleepy appearance and they laid him out in a big armchair for a dozy nap.

Dream-like he nudged himself awake each morning and crucified to his bed he crested his dreams to the windowpane. X-rayed thus, he smiled in glee at the transparency of his subconscious masturbation. He tumbled to his non-ability to function as his body dictated and instead consciously or unconsciously surrendered to mental woding. But one dream puzzled his bleary-eyed scanning. He dreamt he was a window cleaner standing on a rattly silver ladder, and there he balanced clutching his bucket in one hand, his plaid cloth in the other, while with his knees he locked himself to the rungs. The cloth he mellifluously circled in anticlockwise movements. Joy breaded his job, he worked like billy-o cleaning ever widening circles of the weatherbeaten window. As he cleaned the glass he began to look through into the room inside, and to his glee he saw himself reflected in the sunken mirror of his bedroom vanity unit. The all-purpose presses had their doors shut, even the drawers were pushed closed, but the mirror was as bare as the glass before him. Feeling free, he pursed his lips and whistled Nancy Sinatra's 'These Boots Were Made For Walkin'', and true to the words he stood shod in his desert boots. His gaze dwelt on his reflection. He studied his breezy, cheeky face; he watched the circular sweep of his cloth; and suddenly he caught sight of the boy asleep in his bed. He noticed his arms flung wide open, hands relaxed; he breathed visibly, his mouth closed naturally; he had his face turned towards the window, his expression was peaceful; just like a baby he was deeply and happily sleeping. Conscious that he was now looking at himself he stood glued to the ladder. All cleaning stopped abruptly; he even forgot to hold the ladder with his left hand; he was in a trance. How can I see myself, he questioned in his amazement, how can Boyhood be in two places at the same time?

CHAPTER SIXTEEN

A DREAM BEING SHATTERED

SCHOOL frolicked through fifth year and Joseph and his circle of girls and boys made the most of their clubbed disobedience. Paul Browne lived beside the school and many a free class was spent in his house. There they drank tea, played video games or just chatted young people's talk. They listened to pop music or discussed the top of the pops. Then with a fright they'd realize they had overstayed their time, and with some students pushing and some pulling, they'd race Joseph's wheelchair between them back to school in time to save their hides. But like all good things, fifth year slipped away and now here they all found themselves in their final year in Mount Temple.

But sixth year had its attractions too. The headmaster and class tutor jumped on the floor, trying as they were to instil sense into the rabble before them. They pointed out the pitfalls of leaving everything too late, of neglecting to turn up for study, neglecting to be methodical in their preparations for the Leaving Certificate examination, but it was no use at all – time was plentiful and time was on the students' side. After all the outing to Kerry dangled before them, and girls and their boyfriends were planning wild times ahead.

Mount Temple School brought sixth year students on an outing to Dún an Óir each October. Following a grand tradition of guiding their pupils to view their roots and their culture from a broad perspective, they brought them to this Irish speaking area of Co. Kerry.

Prior to the trip the teachers set about preparing the ground.

They gave talks about the geographical, historical and cultural aspects of this great scenic gaeltacht* area. They showed slides of washed sandy beaches, cast exquisite scenes of mountains drenched in filtered sunlight, revealed architectural designs of archaeological sites dating as far back in time as 2000BC, and by crowning their great slide show with marvellous pictures of the clown-faced puffin, the albatross-winged gannet, the fashionable heron and the greedy guillemot, they fired a burning interest in the heart of each of their students.

The teachers set Joseph's heart spinning with excitement when they invited him to come with them on their great planned outing. He decided not to miss out on this voyage of discovery. He was as ready for hardship as anyone else on the trip and he was more than ready for the fun which he detected was in the air all ready and waiting for this gang from Mount Temple.

As usual the teachers cared for their students in every way. They divided them into groups of girls and groups of boys. To each group was allotted a bothán or chalet and one teacher was placed in charge of its inhabitants. Before leaving Dublin the students were assembled for a final rundown of travel arrangements, necessary clothing, living accommodation and the number of the bothán allocated to individual groups. Mr Medlycott laid it on the line that any pupil misbehaving in Kerry would be placed on a train for Dublin, and he stressed that he'd be waiting for them at the other end. Prior to allowing her pupils to go home for a good night's sleep, Miss Henderson clapped her hands for attention and said, 'Now remember please, no latecomers – the coaches leave sharply at nine o'clock. It's a very long journey and we plan to get to Dún an Óir for 6pm.'

Rain deluged down on the morning of departure. Wearing raingear the teachers and students assembled in the dining hall of Mount Temple. The rain didn't deter anyone – after all anything was better than school – and for all that anyone cared it could indeed be snowing. Everyone was going to enjoy themselves and rain cast a damper, but not a mantle over the assembled students.

*Irish speaking.

Coachloads of boys and girls left Dublin en route to Dún an Óir (Golden Fort). Music blared from the radio. The coaches were comfortable and headrests were nicely situated if passengers needed to sleep. But the driver's young charges were fully alert and their sense of anticipation kept them wide awake. Trees fled by the windows, buildings got but a glance, torrential rain battered against the sides, but inside the coach cocooned its bounty in warmth and music.

'We stop at Nenagh for half an hour,' announced the teacher Clive Byrne. 'But make sure you all get back in time,' he said. 'No delays please.' Clutching bags of vinegar-sprinkled chips, cans of soft drink and assorted snack bars, all the students wandered back chewing and rummaging in their nosebags. How Joseph envied them; youthfully he kicked at his handcuffs, for his stomach was crying out for food and the smell of the chips was driving him mad.

Peering through the steamed, rain-rippled windows Joseph was looking for brightness in the evening sky. Approaching Tralee, he was delighted to note that the town was busy for the rain had stopped. Cheering on the sun he looked away towards Conor Pass and Dingle, and as though not to disappoint him the sky grew all the while ever brighter. The coach cruised along, eating up the road to Dingle. Eventually the driver wound his way around a foothill and there, solemnly sitting in a frame backed by three peaked mountains called the Three Sisters, Joseph got his first glimpse of the clustered bothán settlement beautifully dolmaned in a brave sharp sunlight. Smerwick Harbour stretched away to the left, its bulldog wars of old a legend now, for history stiles a path but a people climb across and build a road.

Jesting her pupils, munificent in her caring, Miss Henderson beckoned them to sit down to a royal banquet. She had driven ahead of the coaches and there with Dorothy Siney, Aileen Craig, Donald Moxham and Albert Bradshaw, had combined efforts to cook a lovely hot dinner for the now hungry and weary travellers. Food never tasted better nor was more appreciated, but more surprises were in store. Arriving in his bothán Joseph saw a fire burning on the hearth, food stored in the fridge and water heated for the showers. Everything had been thought about and comfort was but of the making.

School hours established a routine, but nobody minded for each day was fun-filled and busy. The city folk imbued with urban values were now being unwound and for most of them it was a new experience. They looked through city-sighted eyes, but they saw nature at its work pinmarking noble secrets in Dublin students' awareness. Joseph too sat and looked anew at a Kerry full of changes. He drew comfort from the cragged remains of early Irish homesteads and as he sat one evening scanning his surroundings, he noticed a silent rainbow curving an arc across the golden stronghold beside Smerwick Harbour and, momenting awhile, the rainbow then stole away and hid its head behind the Three Sisters.

Each morning students assembled to be briefed on the day's itinerary. The first day saw the loaded coaches pull away for a great day exploring an area which conserved evidence of megalithic man and his lifestyle dating back to 2000BC. The teachers accompanied their pupils and drew their attention to the megalithic gallán or pillarstone which marked the burial site or wedge grave favoured by the early settlers on the Dingle Peninsula. Sitting listening to Donald Moxham fusing his students of history, Joseph heard about the wedge graves being broad at one end and narrow at the other. The graves belonged to the social climbers of their day, and the bodies were usually cremated and the ashes placed on the earthen floor of the grave. Many dead were buried in the same burial chamber, and as though wanting to nest the chambers for future generations' view, they lined and roofed them in stone and, leaba-like*, the grave cradled its dead, while over the chamber rested a huge mound of protective earth and stone.

Meandering through landmarked history, the students next day found themselves at a crossroads in eras in Kerry. Christianity didn't come to Ireland till the latter part of the fifth century, but with the passing years came a druidical art of communicating sparse information. It had to do for the most part with script on

*leaba – a bed.

gravestones. The pagans now used hammer and chisel to carve their ogham cypher on their galláns. Great savage stones stood before the wheelchair-bound boy, and there he saw examples of megalithic man's art very clearly 'broidered by the newly chiselled cross of those early Christians.

The jet-aged Dubliners took to the land of their forefathers and great was their interest when they found themselves face to face with the handcrafts of those farmers of yore. Their dwellings were built entirely of stone, and without mortar to countersink each stone, a method of corbelling was invented. The farmers copied the shape of their currach fishing boats and, building their clocháns (beehive dwellings) in a circular shape, they constructed round stone-walled houses with rectangular insides.

The teachers travelled with the students, and each teacher brought strength to bear as they combined to give a comprehensive background to what lay before the students. Ten teachers in all accompanied the pupils on their combined studies week. The erstwhile scholars were rescued from classroom restrictions, and now in this fior* gaeltacht area of Kerry were invited – nay encouraged – to speak in their native Irish language.

Restless for great adventure, Joseph trembled sometimes at the thought of the difficulty involved in getting him as far as he needed to go. With that in mind, he worried when his teacher Clive Byrne offered to carry him as far as Gallarus Oratory. The route to the oratory was a stile-hurdled pathway and the distance was at least a hundred yards. But with a smile the teacher picked up Joseph, and carrying him in his arms he set off along the path. Coming to each stile Joseph felt the grip on him tightening, as with an enormous effort the man mounted the steps. Then with the last hurdle behind him, the teacher and pupil reached the ancient oratory. Breathing very hard now Clive looked at the lad and said, 'Well Joseph, what do you think of this?' He saw the dimpled smile of wonder spread across Joseph's face as he examined the lovely dry interior of the perfectly preserved corbelled building. It came down through time, and time had no effect on

*true.

the pulled-together walls of this stony scenario. Ireland's early Christians certainly knew about architecture as this church proved, standing now as it stood then over a thousand years ago.

Days strataed lovely happiness out and about among the mountains and bays of this glorious county. Night-time too fed students frescoed delights. After dinner the coaches lined up again to bring Dublin boys and girls to the local dancehall for a nightly ceilidh. Joseph was fretting that nobody would feel that he would like to dance, but again his friends were there before him. In his spinning wheelchair he got dizzy as he danced forward and backward and circled around to the lively music. He felt very much part of the scene and as the assembled students danced aon, dó, trí in formation to the tunes of 'The Walls of Limerick', 'The Stack of Barley' or 'The Statue Dance' ('Rince na deilbhe'), he graced the floor with the best of them. Now he invited Helen Sheil to dance 'Rince na deilbhe' with him, but he needed another partner to dance in front of him. His eye fell on Elspeth Henderson, he bowed towards her and she joined the twosome. The dance was progressing nicely, and each time the music abruptly stopped the three moved not an eyelid; everything was going well. Then with only five people left on the floor the mean music stopped, and even though Helen and Joseph managed to stay stockstill, Elspeth spoiled their chances. She managed to stay as still as a resting flamingo, but then losing her balance she keeled over and shamefacedly the three were ordered off the floor.

Even though they danced set dances all night, next day found the Dublin students out and about as usual. Miss Craig drew their attention to meandering rivers, corrie lakes, knived etchings on mountainsides where blighted potato crops had failed and wiped out local families, truncated spurs and ribbon lakes. Carrying on the examination of Conor Pass they looked down into a very deep 'U'-shaped valley. It was silent and lonely-looking and as he gazed down, Joseph tried to imagine Christmas Eve in that solitary house which nestled away down deep in the echoed loneliness.

Joseph was bewildered by the grandeur of this great mountain road. Cut through a mountain and at an altitude of thirteen hundred feet, the defile looked up at the sheer rockface on one

side and the awful frightening drop to the valley on the other.
Man's engineering skills were here a celebration and Joseph certainly appreciated the wonder of his surroundings. Mr Travers
now joined in and drew Joseph's attention to the striae of the
Conor Pass. He showed him samples of saxifrages and the insec-
tivorous Greater Butterworth.

Looking back at the grandeur of the mountain highway, Joseph
counted his blessings. Imagine crippled me being able to experience the magic of that scene, he mused.

The school tour was now on the move again, heading this time
for Slea Head. Upon arrival the teachers doled out flasks of hot
soup and bread rolls. Munching and supping, the boys and girls
sat looking out to sea. The scene was spectacular; Joseph didn't
know where to look. All about him was the rarest beauty. Behind
him Mount Eagle carpeted a route to the heavens, while the cliff
face before him dropped sheer rock carpet down to the sea.
Looking out then into the blue-hued Atlantic, his eye fell upon
the Blasket Islands as they sat dipping their toes in the cream-
lustred foam of the breaking ocean currents. Overhead screeched
querulous seagulls, as cavorting and gliding they scrambled in
festival. Now and again a dollop sound could be caught as,
Concord-nosed, a great gannet dived suicide-fashioned into the
ocean. The boy sampled a couple of mouthfuls of soup, but his
eyes were busy scanning the Great Blaskets from his height of
several hundred feet.

Beneath him the ocean slurped and backed away, but the
Blaskets seemed to ignore the worrying sea currents, there they
enthroned themselves, silent, proud, seemingly asleep. The largest
island of the group, the Great Blasket, lay nearest to the shore, its
fields and ruins clearly visible. Decked in casted rock and emerald
green, the island claimed fame by producing three native authors.
Their writings were judged unique, for they had broken from a
Homerian-styled oral tradition and, seen through their eyes and
ears, their culture was now for the first time recorded in written
words of their own Irish language.

One of the authors was a woman and her book was on the
school curriculum. Joseph knew her writings very well, but

freshness cast more meaning now that he could see the island of her heart and the sea of her nightmares. Peig Sayers told her autobiography but it seemed quaint and lonely to him and his class, belonging as they did to the nuclear age, the age of science fiction made factual. Now though he judged her human achievements, he admired her serenity, her bravery in the face of fierce fever, sad deaths of husband and children, and seeing the isolation of her home, he felt for her faith in providence despite the awful cracks in fate's charms.

Coping with the extra work and responsibility, the teachers worked as a team. They depended on willing pupils chipping in to give a helping hand, so boys peeled spuds, girls prepared fruit salads and desserts, while the teachers themselves did the cooking. Conversation and laughter marked each mealtime, while at night open house was declared by Donald Moxham's invitation to 'just lift the latch.' The students taking up the teacher's invitation went ag bothántaíocht, and sitting around a blazing fire they drank tea, told yarns or sang songs just as did their ancestors before them. Joseph revelled in visiting assorted bothán owners but in his gladness a music of bodhran-beat broke into his soul. He watched new joy beat its way into the hearts of his classmates, a joy which defeated gloom by dubbing their merits with a first glow of bashful amethyst hue. He never sobbed upon his loss, but cemetery dampness clung in the air as he watched boys pairing off with girls and girls while masking yes beamed no, meaning gigglesome maybe.

Fashioning desire into lonely acceptance was ever the solution to maimed life, so as he gunfired Boyblue's beardless smile he now turned his gaze towards Dublin. It was final night in Dún an Óir, and Joseph Meehan was dipping his headlights on the Three Sisters and swinging his beam around to focus it on the last kick in Kerry. It was the teachers who put on the entertainment for their students and as the party progressed, the boys and girls felt at one with the staff. 'Did you ever hear Clive Byrne singing "An Puc ar Buile"?' whispered Paul Browne, and Joseph shook his head and suggested that Paul should request his teacher to sing it for the assembled group. Paul waited his chance, and then Joseph saw his friend talking with the teacher. Clive Byrne glanced down at Joseph, while Joseph sat bowing his coaxing enquiry up towards the teacher. Paul arrived back and whispered, 'I think he's game, just wait till he's hyped up.' True to his form Clive stood before the assembled students, and wearing an Aran geansai he sang his sean nós rendition of the old Irish ballad 'An Puc ar Buile' ('The Raging Goat'). Everyone applauded and the lads whistled their ear-shattering whistles while Joseph laughed his boyish laugh at the spectacular unaccompanied singing of the old traditional song. He deeply appreciated Clive's bravery in obliging him, for the boy felt sure that in order to sing a song like that a man needed a wet whistle and a pint of Guinness standing by to dampen a throat.

Night-time in Kerry freezes blackness into giant fears, so final night in Dún an Óir held demon black by the tail when Mr Travers told his grizzly ghost story. All lights were switched out; just a lone candle burned. The storyteller's voice hushed everyone into complete surrender. Building up fear he hurried his demons along, and then at the crucial moment of terror the damn candle heeled over, frightening the living life out of his raw-nerved audience. They let out a demented scream, then all scrambled to regain composure, for at that precise second the lights suddenly switched on to reveal chilled expressions on the students' faces. All faces broke into embarrassed smiles – for who would believe in a ghost?!

Voices woke the boy next morning, footsteps moved hither and thither on the paths outside. Folk stood at their half-doors chatting to their neighbours. Everyone was ready for the return journey to the city. Helen collected Joseph and together they made their final round to each bothán resident.

At noon the silver coaches pulled away from the group of holiday chalets in Dún an Óir. The students, all quiet now, took their private farewells of the sunny setting. The drivers drove carefully along the narrow lane, bumped over the little bridge and then changed gear on the straight stretch. Joseph jeeped up and down, trying as he was to create magic from the scene. He looked back at his bothán, looked again at the sea, looked at the white horses spanking a protruding rock outcrop, and desperate to store his framed picture he glanced hurriedly at the Three Sisters. Bowing towards them he bade farewell, but he grinned his mischievous grin before they disappeared from view. I'll be back, he warned, I'll be back. You three may have slept in repose while I saw a dream being shattered. As he descried his farewells he determined to back his resolve. Sleep enveloped his fellow students and in no time he felt sleepy too. His was a tired body, bold yes, but weary now. New experiences crammed his mind, and boy that he was, his body fretted away his energy despite it being but his shell.

Lollying heads rested in weary pose when the driver brought his coach to a halt in Nenagh town. 'You know the rules,' announced Clive Byrne. 'All hands back here in half an hour.' But his students didn't even need reminding, they were looking forward to getting home to Dublin, while strange to say, their conversation still dealt with Kerry.

Evening gave way to night, feeding umber-toned colours into the city skyline. Joseph sat looking ahead towards sonorous Dublin. He felt sly by being seen to miss Kerry but as he drove through Inchicore, past the Oblate Church and down the hill past Heuston Station, he was beginning to doubt his feelings. The coach driver eased his bus into the northbound stream of traffic and crossed the lovely lamplit Liffey. It's a different planet up here, mused the boy, it's day and never night. No place here for ghosts, he smiled, it's Molly Malone territory. He glanced out through his window and saw himself looking in, but now other faces crowded into his mirror. He named them but really he didn't need to, for they were all the sons and daughters of that woman of this fair city. Look, he jeered himself, look, not a country bumpkin among them. He bothered himself with teasing, but inwardly he felt just like the rest of the rabble.

Joseph tried to stay awake that night; he wanted to look back on his days in Dingle. He wanted to savour his mumbled chubby findings but sleep nudged his milestones into subconscious meanderings.

CHAPTER SEVENTEEN

KERNELLED LONELINESS

SCHOOL outing to Dingle now over, it was back to business in Mount Temple. Irish class was first subject that afternoon and the lads brought the rugby ball into the class. They were all waiting for their teacher to arrive, but boys being boys the match between Mount Temple and Columba's came under discussion. 'We'll do a bit of reverse passing,' said Paul Browne and so saying, the four team members took up position. Gary Gilbert passed it back to Stephen Monahan, and he passed it to Roger Stanley, and he in turn passed it to Paul. Now they built up speed, and with the class ducking and swaying out of line of the lively oval rocket, great fun was being had by all. Joseph was in his element, as time and time again the ball whizzed past his nose. Faces, grabbing hands, excited breathing was all about. He felt so much part of the scene, he loved the mêlée, loved being in the middle, loved the sense of movement and teamwork. 'Let's put a spin on the ball, it always makes the reverse pass look more spectacular,' suggested Gary. The lads got set, Gary's body spun with the spin, but the spinning ball soared ceilingwards. Right on target it struck the long tubular light. Crash and down fell a shower of white dust, long splinters of glass and fragments. Right on top of Joseph it landed, but for once his body obeyed and he too managed to duck. Paul, Roger and Stephen bent down, and resting their hands on their knees they rocked with merry laughter while poor Gary stood transfixed, mouth gaping open, looking up at the guts hanging from the light fixture. Joseph burst out laughing as glinting fragments fell from his hair. 'God, Gary that was some pass,' said laughing Stephen, and Gary, desperate to explain said, 'I didn't mean for the friggin' thing to go so high.' The whole class were now as one and together the girls and boys began to pick up the glass. 'Ssh, here's Byrne,' whispered someone, and before they could even think of an excuse, Mr Byrne the Irish teacher stepped in to frown his enquiring look. 'What's going on here?' he demanded. 'It's my fault, sir,' said Gary, 'and I'll pay for the damage,' he offered. The teacher glanced at the oval ball which lay on the floor near his feet, looked at the blitzed ceiling, looked at the scared faces of the entire class and fashioning his sternest expression he said, 'Clean up this mess. Paul Browne, take Joseph to the cloakroom and remove the glass from him and his chair. Now everyone else down to the dining hall. Gary Gilbert, come with me and you can explain what happened to the Head. He may let you off and he may not. Can I be sure it was an accident?' Gary was desperate as he said, 'God yes sir, we were only practising some passes and the ball went too high.' 'Well, come on then,' said the teacher, 'and I'll see what I can do for you.'

School colours on match day represent artillery in supporters' hands. Mount Temple's azure-blue and black striped scarves were for waving and threatening. Each pupil was of a mind to help his own team to victory, and by the hundreds they trooped towards the pitch in Castle Avenue. The match was the Pennant Final against St Columba's College. Decidedly anxious for his pals, Joseph sat watching his pack squaring up to their fancied opponents. He hurt when he saw the scrum-half kick a great penalty goal for Columba's. Sitting near the touchline, he listened to the rival supporters screaming and roaring. He was swearing and cursing under his breath, but when Stephen kicked a thirty-five yards' penalty goal he wished yet again and in vain for a voice. He was all the time waiting for a Mount Temple try, he couldn't care less about Columba's lovely controlled play – he could only see Nico, Mono, Greg, Gary or Paul, and when he was joined by Mr Medlycott he heard him roaring on the lads just as he would wish to do himself. Columba's were in a commanding lead, but John Medlycott was running every run of the ball with Mount Temple and Joseph couldn't help smiling at the grown man giving his senses for a band of schoolboys. But when the crippled boy had given up almost, didn't Roger Stanley burst over the line for a spectacular try for Mount Temple. But then didn't the final whistle blow any chance of a conversion. They were beaten by a more experienced team, but their coach Clive Byrne was loud in his praise of his school's fight to the whistle.

Healing from defeat, the lads continued to practise. Long discussions took place out in the smoking nook at the back of the science block. Joseph sat listening to their plans, arguments and strategies. It was typical March weather, the east wind blew fiercely gnawing at his fingers and nibbling at his ears. He sat amidst his friends and as they grew colder they worried about him. Making a circle around him, they sheltered his frail body from the biting winds. Sometimes they tucked his numb-cold hands into their own pockets and while holding them there they tried to instil heat into him.

The lads practised each Tuesday and half-day Wednesday, but Joseph could not be there. However, he assessed how they were coming along by listening to their measuring each others' weaknesses. But now they had another match on the horizon and he heard them planning how best to close apparent gaps in their play. Paul was worried about his boots and he said he was going to buy new studs. 'I've the last class free,' he said, 'and I'm going home to get some money. Then I'll slip down to Fairview for them.' Game Joseph was first in. He looked at Paul and hinted, 'Can I come with you?' Paul smiled and said, 'Are you free for last class?' Joseph shook his head, but hinted, 'Can I come anyhow?' 'It's OK with me,' laughed Paul. Then Stephen chipped in. 'Can I come too?' 'Me too?' said Ben Simpson, and class or no class the four set off for Paul's house. Paul's mother was more than a little surprised to see the four hardies setting off for Fairview, but they all looked back at her and laughed at her seeming concern. She laughed too and shook her head before closing the front door.

Delighted with his friends' loyalty, hackneyed by the strong willing hands of Stephen, Joseph felt himself being trundled along towards the sports shop. The boys chatted comradely, they hassled girls whom they encountered on their way home from school, they bought cigarettes and lit up, and they kindled anew the spark of happiness in their passenger's mind. The wind was piercing through each of them but it was their pal in the wheelchair whom they worried about. Stephen had a brainwave, and stripping his red scarf from around his neck, he wrapped the still-warm scarf around Joseph's cold throat. Then all four, sporting only sweaters and one scarf, breasted ahead again towards Merville Avenue. The shop 'Little Sport' supplied Paul with the studs for his boots, while outside Ben, Stephen and Joseph examined the great display of new bikes. The able lads discussed the pros and cons of individual models, but on looking at the price tags they good-naturedly laughed at the futility of their appraisal. Shopping completed, they sauntered along and then suddenly Paul looked at his watch and said, 'God will you look at the time.' Looking at Joseph he said, 'Now look where you are, and your Mam is above in school searching around for you.' Joseph laughed at the thought of Nora meandering about in search of her son. He knew she would find out without bothering a teacher. She knew his friends and she'd know whom to ask. But they'd brought Joseph with them and the lads were concerned about his being absent from the school, so Paul gripped hold of the handles of the wheelchair and said to Stephen, 'Let me take a turn and we'll make tracks.' Joseph's teeth rattled as his chair bumped up and down off the footpaths. Gasfired by Paul's kindness and Stephen's heat, he gasped with mummified feelings of fortune. Racing along, they had no time to smoke or hassle girls, they were hell-bent on getting to the school before Nora got worried. But they didn't know Nora like he did. Turning in the gate of Mount Temple, whom should they meet but Nora strolling along she was, on her way to meet them. She started to laugh when she saw the lad with the scarf. She felt for the caring which the boys displayed, and humbly she thanked them for the gleam they put in Joseph's eye.

Nora measured hasbeens in her son's life, but how was she ever to know the schemes devised by his friends in school. Bashful boys were uninhibited when adults were out of the way. Meeting after class, his cabby-drivers clubbed together to have rides on his wheelchair. Standing Ben-Hur-like they rested their feet on the low shafts at the rear of the chair, and steering it by the handgrips they hurtled down the schoolyard hill. Joseph sat strapped in in his phaeton whilst his joyful rider screamed, 'Charge', and, 'Get down on your haunches Joseph, we're fightin' men', and, 'Let able-bodied blokes fuck out of our way.' Delightful fun was commonplace and passengers grew in number. Standing room was exploited to the limit when the wheelchair was asked to carry five pals. The five chums positioned themselves as best they could. Wasting not a spare inch of bars, the boys found footholds and with Joseph seated in the passenger seat, the fellows stood one hanging on either side, one acting as driver, and with the fifth seated on Joseph's lap the fully-loaded gazebo laboured at first, but eventually picked up speed. Such was the scene as the headmaster rounded the corner, and such was his telling-off that the chair rarely carried more than three passengers on crest-runs of the future.

Brash boys brought normality into limb for gombeen Joseph. Fresh-faced girls injected happy laughter into that normality and Mount Temple brought fond meaning into the lonely arras by greeting numbness with understanding. The life of Joseph Meehan breathed terrible havoc, but he found comfort through the brotherhood of his friends.

Stephen whacked his pal on the head with his school satchel one day and whispered, 'I'll bring it in tomorrow.' He had earlier told Joseph about this smashin' magazine which he had at home. He wouldn't say what it was about, but built up his pal to such a height of mystery and expectation that he could hardly wait to see it. Next day he purposely sat beside Joseph saying, 'See, I remembered you,' and surreptitiously drawing the magazine from his satchel, he propped it up against the back of the fellow in front. Joseph, keen with excitement, looked at the full-colour picture of the most perfect specimen of manhood he had ever seen. He burst out laughing. He couldn't stop, of all people to be chosen he reasoned, his looking at a bodybuilt stallion of a man was like a pinkeen eyeing up a whale. Stephen was puzzled and embarrassed by his pal's reaction, but undaunted he turned the pages for him. Joseph saw men oiled and roped with muscles, as standing in model poses they forced biceps and other muscles to spring forth from places where he doubted he had a muscle at all. Joseph couldn't explain why he found it so funny, but somehow Stephen sensed that this magazine was not what Joseph expected. He made the best of it by saying, 'OK, so you weren't impressed,' but then he warned, 'I'll show it to your mother if I meet her today.'

Such was the fun and such the normality of school life in Mount Temple. Stephen's magazine was but the quirk of one day – the next brought something else. Joseph was in his biology class, while up at the blackboard Mr Shackleton was drawing a diagram of the reproductive system. Down in the back row he sat beside Greg, and on the other side of him sat Rosemary and Dawn. Rosemary was twiddling a ring on her finger when Greg grabbed it from her. He examined it and tried it on his own broad fingers, but failing to find a finger slim enough, he grabbed Joseph's hand and slipped the ring on his middle finger. It felt grand for a while but with the tightness of his clenched fist, the finger began to swell on either side of the ring. Joseph showed it to Rosemary and she tried to remove it. The finger got red and swollen. Dawn tried her best but it wouldn't budge. Greg said, 'Let me at it,' but it was no use. Rosemary kept whimpering, 'Give me back my ring, Joseph Meehan, that ring has great sentimental value.' Joseph tried to shut her up. Now Mr Shackleton was looking puzzled but he didn't interfere. The threesome moved over to the sink and got at Joseph with the soap. The ring wasn't budging and Joseph had visions of his finger being sawed off. After an almighty struggle, Greg managed to force the ring over Joseph's knuckle and then peace reigned again. 'Now can I have your attention. Please,' said Mr Shackleton. He seemed to have detected what was going on and decided to keep on teaching. He was that sort, he never created hassle where trouble was taking care of itself.

Fronds of fused fire designed by Mr Keogh decorated the sand-marked, blocked walls of the art room. Long trestle tables stretched the length of the area. Seated on high stools, his students drew and painted under his friendly tuition. Joseph gazed at his teacher, he watched the way he guided his young protégés. Gobbling saneness in this class, the crippled boy became a silent still artist. He sat and painted vast canvasses, rescuing life by bringing it alive in garlanded, sly-beaded boldness. Deciding what to draw was never a problem. Creating vast scenes of lonely desert brought him bang up against despair, but by fecundscaping the desert with cone-shaped pyramids, humpbacked heavily-laden camels being fondly led along by bright-robed Arabs, binding nomadic nature to bungled needs, he clustered brilliance of nature inside man's mind despite adverse husbandry. Tired from his mental efforts of redressing his decided moiderdom, he glanced towards the triumphs of his classmates. He killed his desire to bypass them by hoodwinking himself that society was not nobbled by boyish failure, but was in fact enamoured by his boy's fight to bring geared failure to its sleazy knees, and grandly drawing strength from all manner of fronds he sacked his silent desert of its anointing.

Comforted by schoolboys' blunt backing, Joseph nested disappointments in his boy's heart. But he had blunt backing affectionately bestowed on him too. Gunfired friendship momented first by his sister Yvonne, now encompassed him bossily inside a circle of girls of all ages and no age. They banished his cur-image and noisily grunted gladness in his husband falsehood. Youthful though he was, he had long ago snapped shut his challenging, fees-fashioned future and humanhinded his woldway as a celibate pilgrim through life. Tickling his fancy always was the image of the breadbreaker's calling. Priest-named, his fatherhood could be measured just as though he clasped healing power in his kernelled loneliness. Banished dreams always healed in the presence of God. In his Christian yearning for service, he bread-filled himself and his soul each time he received the sacred eucharist. Versed in service to his brother man, his priest-uncle continued to bring communion to him each Sunday afternoon. Basted now by grace, his gabbled verse fused appeals for bygones of hurt feelings; answering from distance and direction, voiced fasts now breathed blessed, thistled relics of relief.

CHAPTER EIGHTEEN

ACADEMICS' THESAURUS OF THOUGHTS

FINAL year was now in its final countdown in Mount Temple. Joseph was looking now towards his future. Lying in his bed, his eye fell many a time on a poster on his bedroom wall. It showed a great new dawn birthed in brilliant new sun, while in its path of laser light flew a pointy-beaked black bird. Words from Psalm one hundred and thirty-nine framed its message: 'If I take the wings of the dawn and dwell at the sea's furthest end, even there your hand would lead me, your right hand would hold me fast.' In time a decision was made, and in making that decision Joseph decided to talk to his headmaster.

'Mr John Medlycott, will you act as a go-between regarding me and my wish to study at Trinity College,' wrote Joseph on his typewriter. He was in his final month at Mount Temple and bedamned though he was, he wished to test himself and his chances at university. He feasted on geared life in secondary school and planned now to pursue his course in third level education. Can I do it, thersed umbilical-tied Joseph. Can I break free from my bondage? Very likely I'll stagger by the wayside, screaming non-voiced screams for help and understanding. Perhaps I'll be frozen academically by the genius of the mitred staff. Can cripples like me be daft enough to expose their handicap? What will I do if students ridicule me? Beast-like in my henpecked life, will I come across as a nancyboy when eddies flow quite current-normal within blasted, handcuffed normality? Must I go public as hell, yet silent as heaven's vastness? Can my family take on the challenge? Can a cripple drain the last drop from the bleeding heart of his family? Kind they try to be, but you know their cross, you know the fee. What if you fail after a month, what a year? Maybe you shun victory in case of failure – market fashioned fraildom and count the cost.

Painting one of his many cackle-voiced canvasses, he was schooling himself for refusal in Trinity. He was sitting near the door of the art room vying with his present and his future. Painting with his mental crayons, his colours were running amok on him. Why damnwell use purple for the horizon he chided, why not orange or golden yellow? He tried to seize hold of the golden crayon but it slithered from his grasp. He clenched his fingers on the next crayon, but when he saw the colour he cast it from him, trying as it were to hurl black into the very voiceless void of creaking dreams. Why can't I grip the yellow crayon he pondered, sure I can't paint a peace-filled setting sun in red or turnip-blue or burnt black. Zoomed, fast capers loosed some other colours but failure to secure hold on golden yellow voiced dashed boyish sighs from his sad soul. Crayon caught now he filled in the game, golden horizon, flushing it by streaks of stirring turnip-blue, vivid red shots and hues of storm-mobile black. Desert carrion-flies droned all about his landscape, beast-cruel they joyfully nibbled at his placebo, but brashly he shooed them off lest they might puncture his confidence.

Joseph sat silently viewing his efforts, peeping now and then at the door, but still he was caught unawares. His body jumped when the door handle turned, his head jumped back on his shoulders, he quickly examined the face of the headmaster. The step of Mr Medlycott was firm and definite. His features gave nothing away. He strode over to Mr Keogh and said, 'Can I have a word with Joseph Meehan? I'll bring him outside to the corridor.' Looking stern, he returned to seize the handles of Joseph's chair and quietly wheeled him out into the green-painted corridor. Then stepping around in front of his seated pupil he said, 'I've just had a phone call from Trinity College. Yes, they'll accept your application. The professor, a Dr Terence Brown, said they'll be pleased to have you as a student.' Joseph filled to the brim with joy and looking into the now dancing eyes of this noble man he fashioned his bow, bow, bowed thanks. Zealous mercurial dreams were about to be realized and sweetly the headmaster smiled his far-seeing smile.

Boasting greeted his mother when she arrived at lunchtime. Joseph told her his news and asked her was she pleased for him. Nora Meehan hugged her son and said, 'Boys oh boys, have you bitten off a mouthful!' Joseph laughed nervously. Joining in, his mother hugely smiled. Pouring tea from the flask she hushed his nervousness and handcuffing his arms she gave him some hot, strong, sweet tea. Then sitting down she said, 'Now, let's have it. I want every detail.' Sad backing cast from him, he told Nora of his news from Trinity. Catching then her strict attention he indicated that Mr Medlycott wanted to speak to her. 'What time does he come back from lunch?' He told her shortly at two o'clock. Then gathering her flask and her son, she nodded to her boy and wheeled him out into the many-peopled mall towards the cloakroom and afterwards towards the head's office.

Fearful for her son's undertaking she chatted with John Medlycott. He lessened her worry by telling her that two members of Trinity staff were intending to come to meet Joseph in his home. 'Be sure to ask for special attention to be paid to your slow method of typing,' suggested the frank teacher. 'You know Joseph, you'll have to submit a weekly essay and also a lengthy term essay,' instructed his headmaster. Fearful never, but frantic for his handicap, Joseph served up glad smiles in place of frenetic misgivings. Nora Meehan chortled when she thought about her snail-speeded son typing up weekly essays. 'Doing and saying you'll do is a horse of a different colour Joseph, but you brought it on yourself, now it's all up to you,' laughed Nora.

Hymn-filled, Joseph neatly toned his mental hothouse flower, fostering took too much faith in other people. He realized that his musical musings needed constant nurturing and he felt certain that he could count on Trinity to ease his eyes open; he longed to hear how the academics judged grand literature. Assurances now boldly gambolled in his brain and bolstered his ego.

Joseph was dying to share his news with his friends, but Mr Medlycott let him home early. Now I'll have to wait till tomorrow he thought, but then again maybe Paul or Peter will call tonight. Wonder what will they say he fussed, but more importantly what will folk in Trinity say when they see a gombeen gracing their corridors. Crazy you must be joining the academically brilliant he scolded, fool to kiss goodbye to dear old isolation. Imagine going looking for thrills. You'll get your belly-ful my lad – hell hath no fury like scorn for spastics and you go looking for it, asking for it, offering yourself as a human sacrifice. But then again why not go, why not chance it? You're too ready to judge people's motives. Look what you found in Mount Temple – for every rotter there was a dozen right ones, in fact there was a score of right ones, so don't condemn before you even try it out. Play it by ear. Friends will back you up – maybe Paul, or Peter, or Stephen, or Greg, or loyal Helen will help you break the ice, but don't panic, don't be beat before you start, don't be a bloody coward, don't get all steamed up – no one is going to take a bite out of you, more like you'll take one out of them. Oh God, come to think of it, what'll I do if my hands grasp someone by the seat of their pants? They'll just say he's queer – that's what they'll say – bloody queer that fella going for your balls. Jesting of course they'll be, but they'll never know if they don't get to know me and my flailing arms, they'll ... ah shut up, shut up feck off, you have me moidered, just damn well wait and ....

Was that the clock striking, mused the boy, as he drove in along the avenue to Mount Temple. Now the voyage of discovery was at an end. It was his last day in the noble school. His eye glanced gamely over the lovely spired building, glanced up into the just and watching clock, and voicing loneliness for his merry days here, weathering gang warfare and loud laughter, his had been the fun, his the beauty-packed life.

Never assessed as anything but normal by class-clanned friends, he experienced things which he would never tell, saw things which he would never describe, snared life that would last him till the grave, and all because a school said to hell with the begrudgers, we'll welcome Joseph Meehan into our midst.

As gadflies flitted, famished Joseph Meehan mingled amidst students and staff. The Mount Temple garden party was in full swing. Weather scattered class snobs, as dressed to the nines they dashed indoors out of the unseasonal downpour. Damming back sorrow the disabled boy mastered the situation, for he felt that tall boys make tall men and pals branded scholars now would very soon join regular men in nature's great woldwalk. But his pals were out to enjoy themselves, so he folded up his feelings and made the most of his chums' company.

The red motor car passed by the gate; it was moving very slowly. 'I'll bet that's them,' suggested Matthew. Heaving a sigh, Joseph watched the two men walking in along the driveway. Here they are, he cheerfully gasped. Wonder what'll they think he mused, but Nora was opening the front door and saying, 'You're very welcome.' Fashioning a faith in himself he looked into the faces of the two grand professors. He smiled with relief as Brendan Kennelly thumped him on the shoulder and said, 'Howya Joseph, remember we met in Listowel.' The other man followed suit and grasping the boy's hand he shook it warmly. Ceaseless worries reared up and galloped away. Conversation meandered through green fields. School never sounded like this, thought Joseph as he sharply heeded the thoughts and trains of the academics' thesaurus of thoughts. Imagine listening to fellows like them every day he mused; if they can move me by conversation by heaven they must sound good giving a researched lecture. Holding their gaze the boy boldly tossed his eyes towards a typed sheet of paper. It was a typewritten letter in which he told the two men of how he saw himself in the role of student and he highlighted the great, enormous challenge which he felt would be hurdling his pathway through university. Wanting to reassure him, the professors tempered his school of thought by stressing that his brash creativity could well do with a great deal of discipline, and that he would learn in their college and under their tutelage.

Seeing that his school was that very night holding its farewell dinner meant that Joseph heaved a delightful sigh of relief when the great men decided it was time to leave. Frantic worries famished gladly and feelings of honest faith held sway. He bid farewell to Drs Brown and Kennelly and faced immediately for fun and frolics in Howth.

With a lissom débutante resting a hand on their shoulder, the boys graced the dancefloor of The Royal Howth while caesuras associated with loneliness filmed across Joseph's creativity or life. He longed to be bedded by boldness but settled instead for deaf-noted friendship. Seated in their midst he marvelled at falseness and sanity. Blessed girls made sure he was included in the dancing, the drinking, and the dull banqueting. Freedom from flings fitted him out for the role which he played; he was everyone's confidant but nobody's fool. Plastered by success as a juvenile poet he hesitated not in mulling his wine, peopling his knolls with fare flung at him from off the wheel of fortune, and building on those ingredients he cackled bonnie fairness from out his haunted soul.

Dancers took the floor for every dance but not everyone was cut out for dancing. Fellows flagged after a couple of breathfired flings whilst Joseph twirled on the floor like the chairoplanes in a carnival. Feeling dizzy but undaunted he swirled about, flashing lights speeded by, schoolfriends gyrated at enormous speed – gullible Joseph was judged to be having the time of his childish life. But having the time of his life he was having, for contrary to his friends' interpretations he saw girls' invitations to dance as their sad but last chance to show him that they had really cared all along. The combination of attention from boys and girls stirred the crippled boy's soul. He greatly admired their differing approaches and as he sat with them watching them eating their school's farewell dinner he chewed mentally on the food of frankness. But drinking was a different desire. He swallowed beer, vodka Martinis and Dubonnet until life became blissful and hell acceptable. Schoolfriends found the going tough, they found walking difficult, but Joseph had no such worries. He sat at his ease, a broad grin fixed on his face; he certainly couldn't wipe it off, and he thought fame came when a fella can't stop smiling.

Dawn was filtering the eastern skyline as Joseph Meehan, smiling still, made his way home. His father drove carefully, but his son cast glances heavenwards. Why can't he get a move-on thought Joseph. Sampling desperate freedom the cripple now wanted to fling off his cloak and sack handicap of schottischestepped, brazen bric-á-brac.

Nora laughed, she giggled and hesitated. Assessing her disabled son's mean smile brought laughs lightly from her heart. Settling her son in bed she said, 'God help him in the morning – leave the phone off the rest – he'll not want to hear noise for at least a week.' Matthew laughed too but Joseph wondered why.

CHAPTER NINETEEN

HIS HUMAN WASTELAND

WHACKY-NESTED notions about fledglings needing time to practise their writing skills went straight out the window when Joseph Meehan went to Trinity College. The boy found himself bending his ear to the fashionable greats in literature. Now he was being challenged by Brontë, Dickens, Conrad and Sterne while dramatists like O'Casey, Beckett and Synge kindled munificent mullings in his ribald mind. Feasibility cased him in silence but breathing noisily, he brought his total concentration to bear on what the lecturers were saying. He bashfully sat amongst brilliant, vocal students and marvelled at their shyness and their youthful inhibitions. They banked great mentalities but during tutorials they clammed shut oftentimes, leaving Joseph hopping with frustration for their choosing to join the ranks of the mute.

Turning from being a boy-writer, undisciplined and gauche, to his new role of student having to write a weekly essay in practical criticism, made Joseph best his handicap and his less than acceptable writing speed. Sack-filled with ideas, he nested his consciousness until the date for surrendering the essay was nigh, then when the gun was to his head he got down to his writing. Certain brands of spasm schooled his body while his mind was attempting to ease out its boldness. His speed was determined by his body spasms and the nearer the date for submitting the essay, the fiercer became the locking quality of each spasm. Nora tried encouraging her son to type his work over many days but although he knew she meant well, he could not convince her of how very difficult it was to choose the right moment to start. Panning for ideas the boy thought and thought. Looking at his work for criticism he was completely on his own. Not for him the great books of critical analysis – he never even saw the Trinity library – but he mentally examined the prescribed Lawrence poem or Hopkins classic and then under pressure of time he collected his creative thoughts, only then to scorn his bedamned spasms which sneakily set about tightening his body in a stranglehold. As deadline of night drew near, so his crippled body drew out its deadliest snares, catatonic-like he fractured his cackling-voiced thoughts by assuming a headlocked stance over his machine, not now able to finish, and he so very near the final sentence. The family grew impatient as they failed to understand why he should be so nervous, and he almost finished. His mother would wheel him back into the kitchen while his student sister Yvonne would try to ease his plight by brewing a cup of coffee for him. But the relaxation would be shortlived. The moment he crossed the threshold of his study, back would come his body rigidity. Nobody could help him, nobody knew what his final sentence was. Nobody could come to his aid, only God, and he was already gone to his slumber. As dawn crept in the windows the Meehans crept up the stairs to bed – their son had eventually cracked the nut – he had mastered his body and finished his essay. Now he too could hand up an essay next day in Trinity.

Bibletrue division existed between joyful-named Trinity and hessian-attired Joseph Meehan. Outward signs belied his brain-power and gobbled his gumption by making his limbs flail foolishly whenever he was close by another person. His family did their utmost to save him from embarrassing himself and others. When he was passing near people the family member pushing his chair steered with one hand while with the other hand they restrained his arm in an iron-strong grasp. Sometimes their best efforts were completely scuffled by seeing his other arm fly loose and strike a grand blow against someone reliably passing by. His family member in charge of his wheelchair always hugely apologized for him sometimes explaining, 'He's sorry, he has no control of his hands.' Folk usually accepted his diluted apology.

'I'll meet you in the arts block and I'll come in through the tunnel,' said Yvonne as she dashed away to catch her bus to Belfield. She had lectures in her university but planned to meet Nora and Joseph for lunch. Not wasting a minute, son and mother rushed from Dr Brown's room and taking the lift they hurried to meet Yvonne. She was there and famished with the hunger she said. Chatting comradely about her lecture the two women walked along, Nora pushing the wheelchair. Joseph listened but was at the same time glancing all around the square. He glanced at the campanile, the chapel, and then his chair heeled back on its back wheels and his eyes gazed up into the autumnal-hued sky. Nora knew that her son's very teeth would rattle while his wheelchair bumped over the cobblestoned square, but by running the chair on two wheels only he got a more comfortable ride. They passed out through the front gates of the college and crossed into Westmoreland Street. A man stood reading his newspaper, sampling the day's hasbeens; he stood legs set apart, deep in renegade language he delved the news reports. As the three drew near Yvonne had to step around the man, Nora's spare hand was holding Joseph's other arm but with lightning speed Joseph's unguarded hand flew in between the man's legs while his fingers tickled all before them. The poor man got the shock of his life and swiftly he turned on his tame attacker. Apologies were offered but the man was too startled to reply. Smartly stepping away from the bucking situation the three grimaced and managed to hold back their wicked laughter. 'That poor man's heart was tested today,' giggled Nora, but Yvonne, putting on her sternest expression, bent down and looking her brother in the face said, 'Promise, no more groping today.' Joseph burst out laughing and with his laugh broke lovely comforting ease. Not able to share the lunch with his mother and sister he plumbed cussed bravery and luck huddled close, as smiling with their fun he slowly drank a cup of beautiful creamy coffee before returning to afternoon lectures in the university's Jonathan Swift Theatre.

Boasted boldness in Trinity College teased Joseph, castrating his foolish facial expression, his loud unsuppressed belches, and his candid but academically mumbled festerings. As he sat and typed his very first term essay real fear gripped his heart. Can I say what I really think, he wondered, or do I serve up what I feel they want to hear. He was writing his thoughts about 'The Briefness of Beckett' but what he said roasted credence by being deemed bashful, castrated man reading what he wanted to hear into Beckett's rolecall to awareness. Rising to the occasion his drama lecturer sensed the validity of Joseph's dangling his can in Beckett's well, but framed scholarship catnapped behind momentous Beckett, and the professor sensed that his disabled student needed time to digest and get to grips with sacred greatness. Saving face by casting his lot in with Joseph, drollness came to the rescue when the academic said, 'I'm glad I gave my lecture before I heard your essay.' When he gave his grade A marking to the crippled boy's term paper, he swore it to be, 'A sparklingly perceptive essay', and Joseph bowed to the expert's opinion.

Quiet classes in critical analysis saw Dr Brown gently rambling through Joseph's creative conscience. He was able to help him see greatness in roving criticism. Accounting for richness in glory-filled poetry he veered the numb voiced boy towards greater understanding. Quests engendered by Dr Terence Brown carried Joseph into fields bedecked with golden thoughts. Poorly the disabled boy typed his broad mind's findings, but the professor never creased his confidence. Perceptively he read between the sparse words and managed to read sufficient meaning out of rescued, fumefired language.

Singing at the top of his voice, Matthew always twisted words around to suit the occasion. This morning it was the turn around for *South Pacific* as he bashfully sang, 'Take my hand I'm a strange whore in paradise'. Joseph was sitting on the toilet in the upstairs bathroom, eyes still closed in sleep. It was six o'clock in the morning. Matthew was making do with the downstairs washroom. All of the family were up because Joseph had a nine o'clock drama lecture in Trinity. Matthew was going to travel to work by two buses, and even though Yvonne had no lecture until eleven o'clock, she too was up because she had to hold her crippled brother safely in his seat while Nora drove the car. Sacked of beautiful sleep Yvonne called, 'Joseph, for God's sake come outa there. Its bad enough being up at the crack o'dawn, what with you in there and Caruso downstairs – sure a poor woman would be better off dead. Anyway,' she banged on the door, 'what's Kennelly's lecture on to-day?' '*The Gunman*', shouted Nora. 'Oh,' said Yvonne, 'I'd like to hear him on O'Casey – maybe I'll wait on for his lecture.' Joseph tried to answer her but too late he heard her thumping down the stairs to the kitchen.

Ghosts of former crippled man accompanied Joseph as he was wheeled along the corridors of Trinity College. Yes he had to deem himself specially blessed in being allowed to school his grand spirit in a scholarly and ancient establishment. Sable-coated by his family, he had thus far managed to attend all his lectures and tutorials. They took turns reading the books on his course for him, and at his request underlined and numerically noted the pages which caught his critical attention. Breathing thanks, he watched the price paid by each member, and thought and wondered regarding the right of any fellow so crippled to grab firmfisted at the coat-tails of his family. They reassured him, but still he worried and wondered.

Very cyclones now blew through Joseph Meehan's mind blowing away his collected boyhood hurts, blowing fashioned breath of spring into his human wasteland. Kinky boy that he tried not to be, he budded mental, hickory-hard gladness in his numb heart. Molestations lunged suffocating gloom, but brave boldness fought back as Trinity tried masking loitering fear for fractured fellows. Cute cuts here and there fitted a beautiful certainty around Joseph's bent body. Nobody made him feel different, in fact he looked often for that former look of rejection in people's faces, but all credit to staff and students, he never found what he was searching for.

Drone-bees bloat themselves on the labours of corolla-attracted, nectar-laden inmates who bung danger in order to build a nation. So too did Joseph; he used everybody for his own ends. By the grim rigours of his family he managed to reach college. Seating himself in the lecture theatres, he bloated himself on knowledge. He lauded Marlowe's *Tamburlaine*; he mastered Shakespeare's glorious sonnets; sat and fought Satan with blind poet John Milton; usured Cathy under frantic Heathcliff's evil guidance; debonair-like he frescoed Mr B. with stoic Pamela yessing and guessing for hours for ever; sexually hulled astride Lawrence and Forster he sought out evidence of gullibility in his own perceptions of lonely reading of literature. Crying hurrah for lilysweet knowledge he frowned at the greatness of Joyce; wanting to emulate him for boyhood's fame, he nadir-aspired to mould his only gift into briny, bastardized braille so that fellows following never had to nod yes to mankind's gastric view that man speechless and crippled must forever be strolling as underlings to the yapping establishment.

Crying frog-green, snotty tears, numb babyhood vied with canned laughter in God's great, dabbed-red canvas. Holding onto human looks, baby Joseph Meehan hummed hell's hymn, now here he was in Trinity College playing brain-powered anthems and pummelling momentous bodyblows to brain-budded, normal man.

Certifying honours-level intelligence, Joseph knew that the college priorities were now satisfied, so when he was invited to study for a degree he thought damn thoughts. Bold, brazen yes became bashful maybe. Assessed posers eased his mind: you know you can survive now so why hesitate; go on make the nymph gremlin-green; have guts; be a man; look the world in the face; you know the professors now; you know the students in your tutorial groups; you know you were getting through to them; but they were all looking on you with pity; nut, they opened their hearts to you; you could find true friends among that bunch; remember Mount Temple – you know the signs of heed; mould them to your needs; come on you can crack it; but think, think of the hours trying to finish the damn essays, and you locked rigid not able to bow an inch to save your life; but didn't you manage: didn't you have your essay next day to throw on the table: it might be slim in volume but you had it, that's the important thing – you bested your body. But really how long would you need to study? Well you could manage one subject each year so you're talking about eight years – eight – great God you'd be fit for the bughouse, eight years Meehan – Meehan you're mad, mad now to be considering it, mad you are with no shadow of doubt – but, no butting. Forget about it. Just heed your better sense – that's if you have a better sense or any sense at all.

Can you find out the postal code for Trinity College? nodded Joseph Meehan. He was addressing his letter to Dr Nicholas Grene, a letter pleading forgiveness for turning down his chance to study for a degree in English and Philosophy. Nora looked up the telephone directory and furnished the information that Trinity was in No.2 area. Joseph bowed and bowed until he had the envelope addressed but then he started to have misgivings. As he still had one more lecture, he grimly nabbed boyish feelings to his chest, for after all he decided, he could not go on, but still he grasped hope.

Thursday was his last day in Trinity College. He sat near the door listening to Dr Brendan Kennelly lecturing on Aristotelian criticism. Seeing the relaxed stance of the students, he too took it easy and just listened to Kennelly's mixture of facts, comic asides and general shock tactics. He had a certain way of surprising his audience by either throwing a question at them or else getting their backs up by belittling their glorious poses. Today was no different, but at the same time it was different, for today would never be tomorrow, today really spelt-out the Last Day for Joseph Meehan.

Feeling chagrin coupled with relief, he was making his way towards the lift. Frigid looks he cast on his grizzly future. He felt different. Why has it to be so very hard yet so very wonderful, he pondered. I'm going to miss this like hell, but I'd be sorrier if I said yes. But as he looked yon he saw Dr Brendan Kennelly. 'Joseph, come down to my room, I want to give you something,' said the dimple-faced academic. Wheeling him along, Nora made small-talk with the professor. Reaching his room then, the noble man picked up a book and opening back the black cover he wrote: 'To Joseph – beannacht* – Brendan'. 'That's a little sample of my poetry,' he said, 'see what you think of it.' Joseph smiled and bowed, bowed and smiled, and in a grand sweep of

*blessings

his right arm he brought forward his hand to shake a final farewell with this ambassador of Trinity.

As Joseph reached the vestibule he saw Matthew and Yvonne. They had planned to meet Nora and himself – him the student that was. The doleful day was not going to be funereal, that was the sort the Meehans were. 'We're going to Bewleys,' chimed in Yvonne, 'and I'm going to treat you to coffee and a big squashy cream bun.' She knew he couldn't eat a squashy bun or any bun, but distraction was her scheme.

Steeling himself he looked at his family – what a bunch he chorused silently, what thought, what their love. Assessing how lonely and lost, numb Joseph must feel, Yvonne seized hold of the handles of his wheelchair and off she set, pushing her brother out along the tunnel towards Nassau Street. But honest Yvonne could not understand why his head hung low in thought for:

> Westwards he trudged,
> Eastwards he scrambled,
> Northwards he stretched,
> Seeming lost he southwards beavered,
> Urtication his grim destination.